Richard Steele

Twayne's English Authors Series

Bertram H. Davis, Editor

Florida State University

TEAS 351

RICHARD STEELE
(1672–1729)
Portrait by Sir Godfrey Kneller.
Courtesy of the National
Portrait Gallery, London.

Richard Steele

By Richard H. Dammers

Illinois State University

Twayne Publishers • Boston

Richard Steele

Richard H. Dammers

Copyright © 1982 by G. K. Hall & Company
All Rights Reserved
Published by Twayne Publishers
A Division of G. K. Hall & Company
70 Lincoln Street
Boston, Massachusetts 02111

Book production by Marne B. Sultz
Book design by Barbara Anderson

Printed on permanent/durable acid-free
paper and bound in The United States
of America.

Library of Congress Cataloging in Publication Data

Dammers, Richard H. 1943–
   Richard Steele.

   (Twayne's English authors series; TEAS 351)
   Bibliography: p. 144
   Includes index.
   1. Steele, Richard, Sir, 1672–1729—Criticism and
interpretation. I. Title. II. Series.
PR3707.D3 1982   824'.5   82–1081
ISBN 0–8057–6837–8   AACR2

Contents

About the Author

Richard H. Dammers was born in New Jersey on May 27, 1943, and graduated as valedictorian from grade and high schools in New Jersey. In 1960 he received a Senatorial Summer Scholarship for a prize-winning essay. In 1965 he received his A.B. in English from College of the Holy Cross, in 1966 his M.A. in English from the University of Virginia, and in 1971 his Ph.D. in English from the University of Notre Dame.

His special interest is eighteenth-century English literature; he has published in the *Notre Dame English Journal, British Studies Monitor, The Library, Papers of the Bibliographical Society of America, Eighteenth-Century Life, Costerus, Review, Rocky Mountain Review of Language and Literature,* and other journals. In 1974 he received a Summer Fellowship from the Folger Shakespeare Library for research on Richard Steele. He has participated actively in the national and regional meetings of the American Society for Eighteenth Century Studies.

He is currently Associate Professor of English at Illinois State University.

Preface

Richard Steele is well known to students of eighteenth century literature. His plays were popular with audiences throughout the century, and his final play, *The Conscious Lovers,* had a major influence on English drama. Even more famous than his plays are his periodicals, for the *Tatler* and the *Spectator* achieved popularity with an extraordinarily wide range of readers. The partnership of Addison and Steele was the combination that made these two periodicals so successful, but Steele in both cases was seen as the primary author.

Although Steele's reputation has been entwined with Addison's since the days of the *Tatler* and the *Spectator,* both writers are individuals whose work deserves to be studied separately. Robert Otten's book on Joseph Addison and my book on Richard Steele attempt to do just that, to examine each author as an individual and to evaluate each author's work separately. With these evaluations perhaps literary critics may overcome the need to compare Addison and Steele in order to determine superiority.

My major theme, appearing in all six of the chapters, derives from Steele's first major work, *The Christian Hero.* Steele explains his perception of the interrelationships of religion, reason, and the passions here, and in my opinion Steele retained this perception with only slight modification throughout his literary career. The *Tatler,* the *Spectator,* and *The Conscious Lovers* may all be understood more thoroughly after a reading of *The Christian Hero.* Steele believed that the passions renovated by religion should lead to beneficent virtue and to a concern with the sorrows and joys of other human beings. *The Conscious Lovers,* I suggest, is to a large degree the dramatic expression of Steele's perception of human motivation initially developed in *The Christian Hero.*

The first chapter, then, is devoted to *The Christian Hero* and Steele's perception of human motivation. The second and third chapters are given to a presentation and discussion of the plays, and the fourth and fifth chapters analyze the *Tatler* and the *Spectator*. The final chapter examines the later periodicals. All of these chapters focus on Steele's themes in order to provide a better understanding of Steele's didactic achievement.

I appreciate the assistance I have received in my work on this book from Illinois State University and the Folger Shakespeare Library. I owe continuing gratitude to Calhoun Winton for his support and example; for the quality of their scholarly work on Steele I wish to express thanks to Shirley Strum Kenny, Rae Blanchard, and John Loftis. To my wife most of all, my gratitude for her continued patience and support.

Richard H. Dammers

Illinois State University

Acknowledgments

I am grateful to Oxford University Press for permission to quote from *The Christian Hero, The Englishman, Richard Steele's Periodical Journalism, The Plays of Richard Steele,* and the *Spectator* and to The Johns Hopkins University Press for permission to quote from *Tracts and Pamphlets of Richard Steele* and *Captain Steele.*

Chronology

1672   Born in Dublin, baptized on March 12.

1677–84   Educated by uncle and guardian, Henry Gascoigne.

1684–89   Educated at Charterhouse, London.

1689   Admitted to Christ Church, Oxford.

1692   Joined Duke of Ormonde's Second Troop of Life Guards.

1695   "The Procession," on the death of Queen Mary.

1700   Verse defending Addison published in *Commendatory Verses*.

1701   *The Christian Hero. The Funeral.*

1703–04   *The Lying Lover,* produced in 1703 and published in 1704.

1705   *The Tender Husband,* opened on April 23. Married Margaret Ford Stretch in April or May.

1706   Wife Margaret died during or before December. Appointed Gentleman-Waiter to Prince George in August.

1707   Married Mary Scurlock on September 7. Appointed editor of the *London Gazette* in April or May.

1709   Began the *Tatler,* April 12.

1710   Resigned from the *Gazette.*

1711   Ended the *Tatler,* January 2. Began the *Spectator,* March 1.

1712   Ended the *Spectator,* December 6.

1713   Began the *Guardian,* March 12; ended the *Guardian* October 1. Began the *Englishman,* October 6. Elected to Parliament.

1714   Ended the *Englishman,* first series, on February 15. Expelled from Parliament. Appointed governor of Drury Lane Theatre.

1715   Elected to Parliament again. Knighted by King George I. Wrote second series of the *Englishman,* July 11–November 21.

1716   Appointed Commissioner of the Forfeited Estates for Scotland.

1718   Death of Mary Scurlock Steele on December 26, 1718.

1720   Published the *Theatre,* January 2–April 5.

1722   *The Conscious Lovers* appears at Drury Lane, with a November 7, 1722, debut on stage. *The Conscious Lovers* is published on December 1, 1722, with the date 1723 on title page.

1724   Retired to Wales in ill health during the summer.

1729   Died on September 1.

Chapter One
The Philosophy of
The Christian Hero:
Ethics, Benevolism,
and Christianity

Introduction

Richard Steele, the son of Richard Steele and Elinor Sheyles Symes Steele, was born in Dublin early in 1672 and baptized at St. Bride's church on March 12.[1] His father was poor and apparently unsuccessful; his mother, with three hundred pounds as her wealth, had been widowed with two or three children. Young Richard's family situation was thus not promising, but his grandfather had been important and his aunt was to be influential. Though poor, Steele's family could claim to be gentlefolk. This was a claim never forgotten by Richard Steele, and he used it often in the later pamphlet wars to defend his reputation. His family belonged to the Irish Ascendency, the Protestant minority that dominated Ireland. For the rest of his life he identified himself with Protestantism.

Little is known of Richard Steele's youth. In *Tatler* 181 there is a description of a young boy at age five experiencing but not comprehending his father's funeral; this has long been taken to be about the death of Steele's father. His mother lived on, but almost nothing is known of her mode of life. The gravestones do not reveal any information about Richard Steele's parents.

Raised to manhood by his aunt and uncle, Lady Katherine Mildmay and Henry Gascoigne, Steele left Ireland forever in 1684 when he registered at the Charterhouse school in London. Two years later Joseph Addison registered at Charterhouse, and one may imagine the beginning of the famous friendship. Outside the school walls political turmoil was increasing; Charles II had died, and his brother and successor, James II, was a Catholic. Although the Glorious Revolution was bloodless in England, Ireland was not so fortunate. With Catholics against Protestants the battle lines were drawn. Perhaps because of James II, perhaps because of family memories, Steele identified Catholicism with subversion and intolerance. He understood the dangers to the Protestants if the Catholic majority regained power; then, as now, religious differences were settled by bullets. Steele's environment caused him to fear the danger of Catholic tyranny and to struggle unremittingly for civil rights wherever he found oppression. Calling himself an Englishman born in Dublin, he aligned his life with the Church of England and tolerance, Parliament and the rule of law, and civil liberties. Fortunately for Steele, life progressed more smoothly inside Charterhouse walls in London; in 1689 he followed Joseph Addison to Oxford.[2]

Steele did not take a degree at Oxford. Instead he joined the army, the Second Troop of Life Guards specifically, in 1692. One can imagine his zest for the active life, as he describes in the retrospect of 28 years his decision to leave Oxford:

> When he mounted a War-Horse, with a great Sword in
> his Hand, and planted himself behind King WILLIAM
> the Third, against Lewis the Fourteenth, he lost
> the succession to a very good Estate in the County
> of Wexford in Ireland, from the same Humour which
> he has pursued ever since, of preferring the State
> of his Mind to that of his Fortune.[3]

A wistfulness, a consciousness of bright-eyed youth about to learn by experience, can be detected. But Steele did not achieve the preferment he desired, and he left the army with understandable disappointment in 1705, thirteen years after leaving Oxford.

Queen Mary's death in 1694 provided the impetus for Steele's first published work, "The Procession. A Poem on Her Majesties

Funeral." His conventionally fulsome dedication to John, Baron Cutts, commanding officer of the Coldstream Regiment, Second Regiment of Foot Guards, earned Steele a commission in Cutts's company. During his time in the Footguards Steele engaged in amorous adventures and received for his trouble a baby girl, born to Elizabeth Tonson, sister of Steele's future publisher. To his credit he acknowledged his child and later brought her into his home. Perhaps because of his experience, or perhaps in spite of it, Steele composed while on guard duty a small volume of moral and religious instruction called *The Christian Hero.* Dedicated to Lord Cutts and published by Tonson, the book is a sincere manual of pious instruction, with Steele as the foremost object of reform. In order to regain the favor of the town, which was not impressed by the serious, moral tone of *The Christian Hero,* Steele wrote *The Funeral* or *Grief à la Mode,* a comedy that strengthened his reputation as a literary man and won him the recognition of King William III for future favor. Unfortunately William died before giving anything substantial, and without powerful family backing, Steele found preferment in the military difficult. Success as a writer came more easily. His second play, *The Lying Lover,* was also well received so that by 1703 he was a well-known literary figure. He realized very early, however, that the path to financial gain was through politics, and he offered his talents to the Whigs. After the failure of his third play, *The Tender Husband,* and the damage to his reputation caused by alchemical experiments that he undertook about this time, he began to focus his efforts more seriously on political life. For the rest of his writing days Steele was an uncompromising Whig.

Steele's devotion to the Whig cause cost him the friendship of Jonathan Swift, who found himself equally devoted to the Tory cause. The last four years of Queen Anne's reign were especially tense, for the Tories were in power, the queen had no direct heir, and the succession of a Protestant monarch appeared to be in jeopardy. Each party launched a vitriolic pamphlet war, and Steele and Swift became public antagonists as each led the propaganda war for his party. In *The Crisis* Steele attacked the Tory ministry for appearing to be lukewarm in its support for a Protestant succession. He, of course, suspected that the Tories would prefer the Catholic James as monarch because of his sympathy for Tory policy. In *The Importance of Dunkirk Considered* he attacked the Tory ministry again because of its halfhearted implementation of the Treaty of Utrecht, which required the destruction of the strategic French port of Dunkirk. Swift's response was rapid and powerful; in *The Publick Spirit of the Whigs* and *The Importance of the Guardian Considered* he ridiculed Steele himself rather than his Whig propaganda. Such bitter division rendered these former friends irreconcilable enemies. After 1714, of course, the battles were over. The Tories lost, and Swift retreated to Ireland; from the victories of the Whigs Steele hoped for financial gain, which, however, never met his expectations.

The years after the death of Queen Anne were disappointing and frustrating for him. He had given himself completely to Whig propaganda during Queen Anne's last four years (1710–14) while the Tories were in power; he had taken abuse from Swift and other Tories and been expelled from the House of Commons. He expected more than gratitude. To be sure, the new king, George I, honored Steele with knighthood and supported him with the governorship of Drury Lane Theatre; but further rewards were not forthcoming. Quarrels among the Whigs brought nothing good to Steele, and even his income from Drury Lane was jeopardized by squabbles with the Lord Chamberlain. In 1718 he lost his second wife as well as his son, and it appeared that he would never get out of debt. By 1720 he was a bitterly disillusioned man.

One of the few bright occasions in the later years was the production of Steele's final play, *The Conscious Lovers*. It was a great success on the stage, despite the criticism of John Dennis. But the success of *The Conscious Lovers* was his final triumph. Although he was still a member of Parliament, he did not participate in debate. His health weakening, he arranged to pay his debts over a period of time, bid good-bye to London, and retired to his wife's estate in Wales, where he died in 1729.

The Christian Hero

The first edition of *The Christian Hero* was published in April, 1701, and the second, revised and enlarged, in July of the same year. Intended by Steele as a reforming tract and moral guide for himself and his fellow soldiers, *The Christian Hero* may appear an odd book today, but it was by no means unusual in 1701. Another soldier, Captain William Ayloffe, had published an essay called *The Government of the Passions* in 1700, one year before Steele's work was printed. "Even the originality which might be claimed for *The Christian Hero* as a reforming tract written especially by a soldier for soldiers would probably be challenged, were the book extant, by William Morgan's *Religio Militis or a Souldier's Religion. Writ by a Field Officer in His Winter Quarters* (1695)."[4] But if not original, *The Christian Hero* is important because it presents early formulations of ideas that would later find their way into the *Tatler, Spectator,* and *Guardian* as well as Steele's plays. Still readable today despite its unyielding sermonizing, for Steele's first major publication it is a remarkable book. His expectation that *The Christian Hero* would, in time, be popular proved correct; it went through eight editions during his lifetime (xxxi). The third edition, which appeared in November, 1710, contains his final revisions.

Steele's primary purpose in *The Christian Hero* is to provide an answer to the claims of Stoic philosophers concerning the power of human reason. For the Stoics, reason is a sufficient guide for the passions, which are the springs or sources of human motivation. For Steele, the Christian religion replaced the Stoics' reason as the guide for the passions, as is clear from his title: *The Christian Hero: An Argument Proving that no Principles but those of Religion Are Sufficient to make a Great Man.* Steele argues that because reason is weak and often incapable of offering adequate direction to the passions, with moral error the unfortunate result, one must substitute the dogma of religion for the dictates of reason. Religion has greater persuasive power because of rewards and punishments in the afterlife and therefore can offer stronger ethical direction than reason. Steele concludes, as he hopes the reader will, that human nature, because of its weakness incurred in the original Fall of Man, needs guidance which can be found only in Christianity.

The Stoic philosophers whom Steele opposed generally used figures from Greek and Roman antiquity to illustrate the power of reason over the vicissitudes of life. Cato, the Roman who committed suicide rather than live under tyranny, is a well-known example of the Stoic ideal. Cato needs nothing outside himself since he is adhering to an unwavering belief in the power of his mind to overcome all obstacles. In contrast, Steele believes that fallen human nature is not capable of right action while depending only on its own resources; Steele's Christian depends upon a formulated, codified statement of dogma for philosophical sustenance in times of crisis.

In order to demonstrate his argument Steele begins with three famous Romans—Cato, Caesar, and Brutus—who were unable, he claims, to cope with crises in their lives. These examples prove the Stoic ideal unworkable. Then Steele offers positive evidence of Christianity's value: heroic aspects in the life of Christ and examples from the life of Saint Paul. The final section of *The Christian Hero* suggests that the greatness or heroism demonstrated by Christ and Saint Paul is available to every individual through the guidance of Christianity.

The first book of *The Christian Hero* examines the lives of Cato, Caesar, and Brutus for the purpose of destroying their usefulness as examples of Stoic morality. Steele opens on the defensive: "Why is it that the heathen struts, and the Christian sneaks in our imagination?" (15) The question is slanted, of course since by heathen he implies Romans and by Christian he means eighteenth-century Englishmen, separated by centuries and all that the imagination can conjure. Steele's argument here is designed for the English soldier who wants to hear of active and heroic lives, not of pietistic works in a cloister. His aim is to make the moral decisions necessary in active lives more appealing in Christ and Saint Paul than in Cato, Caesar, and Brutus. He describes the early Christians as "gallant" and "heroic."

Although Steele claims to examine "the practice and resolution" in the lives of eminent Romans of "action and enterprise," he compares them only at one point: death. This, it seems, is carefully planned for the soldier-reader, since in the Preface Steele praises the soldier's willingness to die for others. If the Stoic breaks down under the pressure of imminent death, the soldier can only scorn that weakness. The example of Christ's humbly accepted crucifixion forms an implicit contrast. In addition, praise of the active life and scorn of contemplation both appeal to the soldier and reflect Steele's own bias. Perhaps most indicative of the tone of *The Christian Hero* is the soldierly metaphor "hard and weary march of human life," which reveals a pessimism about human life and by analogy about human nature. Human nature is unregenerate from the original fall; the pain of existence is as miserable as the sore feet and aching bones after a long and weary march. With this pessimism about humanity Steele reduced eminent Romans honored in myth and story to the level of ordinary suffering people requiring help, guidance, and mercy.

The general observations about the lives of Cato, Caesar, and Brutus inject a negative note into the opening of *The Christian Hero*. Each of these figures exemplifies in a different manner the failure of the Stoic philosophy in the final crisis, death. Cato, first, the man of invincible courage and legendary self-control, instead appears tossed about by anger and fury. His last words to his servants and to his son mock their tender esteem. Before dying, Cato expresses rage, then tears open his own bowels, and rushes out of life with fury and indignation (20). Steele implies that Cato's pretension to stoical resistance of the passions is sham; Cato died from disappointed ambition, a thwarted drive for fame, which is, of course, a universal passion. In death, Cato's mask fell, and his wildly explosive end belied his pretended superiority to fortune.

Steele's second example is Julius Caesar, killed in the Senate by his erstwhile friends. Steele uses language connoting warmth and charity to describe Caesar, with praise for his courage and directness in warfare. Because Caesar is the soldier's soldier, it is Caesar's murderer who exemplifies the failure of reason to control the passions. Cassius, motivated by hatred and ambition, ignoring the existence of any deities, and uncontrolled by reason

or conscience, creates and consummates the plan to murder Caesar. Steele emphasizes the lack of control the Stoic philosophy
exerts over one as evil as Cassius. A philosophy that necessarily
depends on individual choice for all restriction of action places
a great deal of trust in human nature. Steele is not so sanguine;
he believes that mankind needs the institutionalized restrictions
of religion.

Steele's third example, Brutus, offers an interesting contrast
to Cato and Cassius because, as Steele says, he ranks among the
best in pagan ethical standards; he nevertheless falls into the
conspiracy against Caesar. Brutus has no just notion of a higher
law or a higher being to support him. Thus even he, the best
of Romans, because he is dependent on his reason for ethical
conduct, errs. Interestingly, however, Steele is not as concerned
with the act of murder as with Brutus's approval of suicide. He
states:

However gallant this speech [approving suicide] may seem at first sight,
it is upon reflection a very mean one; for he urges no manner of reason
for his desertion of the noble principle of resignation to the divine will,
but his dangers and distresses; which indeed is no more than if he had
plainly confessed that all the schemes we can form to ourselves in a
composed and prosperous condition, when we come to be oppressed
with calamities, vanish from us and are but the effects of luxuriant ease
and good humour, and languish and die away. (32)

Human beings require an external influence to renew a desire
for life in the midst of calamity as well as to guide the stormy
emotions. Brutus commits suicide in total despair at the battle
of Philippi, unable to find solace within himself. Steele closes
with a pessimistic speech on human nature: "We may justly
conclude that whatever law we may make to ourselves . . . is
itself but an artificial passion, by which we vainly hope to subdue
those that are natural, and which will certainly rise or fall with
our disappointment or success" (34). Stoicism, then, fails as a
consistent and trustworthy guide. Where can one turn for help?
Steele's answer is reserved for his second chapter.

The second chapter takes the reader through religious history from Adam and Eve to the death of Christ, all the while proposing Christ's preaching and example as the solution to the weakness of reason and the unruliness of the passions. Christ, by precept and example, can rehabilitate the passions into forces for good. Steele's answer to the question of where to turn is a simple exhortation: "Return to that God, in whose Protection only is our Native lost seat of Rest and Tranquility" (40). To support his contention that Christ offers the only adequate guidance for human life he lists many parables and miracles, with chapter and verse from Matthew noted in the margin. The Sermon on the Mount, for example, provides all the rules of life. Steele emphasizes resignation to the divine will and acceptance of Christ's expiation: man's reconciliation to his deity must by necessity come through a mediator, he says, stressing man's innate weakness and corruption while allowing salvation to be gained from without, by Christ's death.

"It was a great article of our Saviour's business in the world, to bring us to a sense of our inability, without God's assistance, to do anything great or good," claims Steele (48). Such a doctrine firmly reinforces the concept of innate human corruption, of which the source is original sin, Adam and Eve eating of the tree of knowledge of good and evil. From their transgression came all the error and suffering that mankind has since suffered, dominated by the hereditary vices of pride, ingratitude, and love of fame. Although Steele is influenced by Hobbes's egoistic theory in the *Leviathan,* he does not assert that human nature is irredeemable, and therefore he makes religion the distinguishing element between his and the egoistic theory of human nature.

"Human life (by long gradation)," Steele observes, "ascended into an art: the tongue was now to utter one thing, and the bosom to conceal another" (39). As he uses it here, the term "art" takes on the meaning of hypocrisy, and the conclusion is obvious: the reader should return to the clear and accepted truths of religion and to a simpler way of life.

Lest he be misunderstood and considered an enthusiast (one who believes that religion is primarily an emotional and not a rational experience), Steele maintains that Christianity is in no way contrary to reason. The New Testament contains plain, easy, and obvious truths; Christianity is comfortable to reason. Whereas in Chapter One Steele degraded reason as too weak to control the passions, in Chapter Two he restores some measure of respect for reason insofar as it helps mankind to perceive the truths of Christianity. John Locke had recently written *The Reasonableness of Christianity,* and Steele apparently wished to include eclectically by compromise and adjustment as wide a range of Christian philosophy in his tract as possible.

The third chapter of *The Christian Hero* focuses on the exploits of Saint Paul, whom Steele portrays as a swashbuckling, imprudent soldier in the service of religion. Perhaps Paul's heroic magnetism appealed to the typical English soldier stationed in some cold, damp, intolerably quiet fort outside London. Steele recounts Paul's dramatic conversion to Christianity and his subsequent attempts to convert the populace. Paraphrasing selections from the Acts of the Apostles and from the First Epistle to the Corinthians, he keeps his account closely linked to the biblical text, with only the addition of military metaphors indicating Steele's hand.

In the midst of Paul's adventures one detects unmistakably the negative philosophical attitude toward human nature found earlier in the book. The people Paul tries to teach are consistently fickle and untrustworthy; men in power are habitually given to vicious practices. Part of this empahsis on human depravity may stem from Steele's harsh attitude toward the Jews of biblical times, but much derives from his philosophical acceptance of original sin as the permanent collapse of natural virtue. In postlapsarian ages virtue and grace can be achieved only by supernatural means, namely, atonement through Christ's death.

Steele's first defense of women, the first of many in his published work, comes surprisingly enough coupled with praise of the Apostle Paul.[5] Mild and understated, it is linked with a modest defense of the passions, which Steele seems never to think of without thinking of women. A virtuous enjoyment of the passions, under the guidance of religion, he finds acceptable.

Good and intelligent young women, he contends, may comprehend religion and be improved by it, and women deserve rational conversation rather than the nonsense of romances (65).[6]

In the fourth chapter of *The Christian Hero* Steele develops the philosophical lessons to be learned by comparing the lives and deaths of Cato, Caesar, and Brutus with those of Christ and Saint Paul. He assumes a common human nature in which the motive powers or passions are guided by reason and by religion. In selecting his terminology he uses the word "fame" as the universal passion and "conscience" as reason. The spring to action is the desire for fame, whereas the restraint of unwarranted action is conscience. Religion, he shows, is the only certain director for either common man or hero: passions "are best used and improved, when joined with religion; we may rest assured, that it is a stable, sober, and practical, as well as generous, exalted, and heroic, position, that true greatness of mind is to be maintained only by Christian principles" (70).

A significant change in tone has occurred; in the first and second chapters passions, the results of original sin, are to be subdued, and in the last chapter the passions are to be used and improved. At first Steele disposed of the passions as he addressed Stoic philosophy; now in the friendly realm of Christianity he allows the passions the possibility of achieving good through sound religious guidance: "God . . . claims not an utter extirpation but the direction only of our passions" (74). Even the universal passion of desire for fame can be turned to good, says Steele, by changing its object from personal glory to God's glory.

Turning to a new topic, Steele discusses the concept of hero within Christianity, looking in the past at Saint Paul and in the present at King William III. The Christian hero must be composed in suffering and humble in heroic action because all of his experience is dedicated to his deity. For the Stoic such composure would have been dedicated to personal honor. Much of this discussion of Christian heroism is directed to Steele's fellow soldiers, men whose goal is fame in arms. Not unmindful of the opportunity for political flattery, Steele offers William III, the soldier-king, as a contemporary example of the Christian hero.

In conjunction with the belief that personal honor must give way to the love of God and neighbor, Steele presents the first of his many anti-dueling arguments: "To forgive is the most arduous pitch human nature can arrive at . . . ; a coward never forgave" (80). Steele despises dueling because he himself once wounded a Captain Kelly in a duel. After this experience he warns his reading public or theater audience repeatedly of the foolishness of dueling; the main point of *The Conscious Lovers,* claimed Steele, was to teach the audience that a man could honorably refuse a challenge to duel. *The Lying Lover* also contains a dueling episode, and the *Tatler, Spectator,* and *Guardian* denounce dueling often (80n).

Replacing the code of personal honor with obedience to the deity is a first step toward Steele's theory of benevolence, which depends on a disinterested willingness to aid or befriend a friend or an enemy because of love for God. "He that loves others for the love of God, must be unchangeable, for the cause of his benevolence to us is so" (79). Steele hinges benevolence on the guiding power of religion, since, without religion, reason or conscience is ineffectual and the passions, returning to their egoistic paths, stand poised in a Hobbesian state of war. Although Steele's philosophy is strongly pessimistic in strictly human terms, he does not dissociate the human and divine. For that reason he is certain that men can achieve a disinterested, benevolent love for one another. In emotionally charged language he describes benevolent people: "It is not possible for an human heart to be averse to anything that is human"; and "when the heart is full, [the eyes] will brighten into gladness, and gush into tears" (77). Paul's preeminent virtue, charity, holds the first position in Steele's theory of benevolence as well: "Charity . . . opens our bosoms, and extends our arms to embrace all mankind" (77). Mankind's ethical basis, according to these exhortations, is emotional rather than intellectual; Steele trusts religiously tinged benevolence rather than reason to determine the morally correct choice.

The Christian Hero concludes with fulsome praise of William III and ranting denunciation of Louis XIV. Such a conclusion, ensuring the book's popularity, was, of course, good politics. Few could criticize such lyrical praise of King William. Steele's impassioned hatred for Louis XIV, however, appears based on religious grounds: he despised and feared the Catholic position on freedom of action and belief. His life's work as a periodical writer and as a member of Parliament had been a striving for greater liberty of conscience and freedom of action. It is appropriate that his sensitivity for individual freedom appeared in his first published work.

Critical Reception

The first critic of *The Christian Hero,* writing in 1702 in *A Comparison Between the Two Stages,* attempted rather ill-naturedly to belittle Steele's work. One should not be surprised at such harshness, since the *Comparison* mocks almost every play, actor, actress, and stage manager involved in London theater. The anonymous critic alleges that the second edition of *The Christian Hero* printed in July, 1701, which indicated brisk sales, was simply a trick of the bookseller to get rid of an unpopular book. More to the point—given Steele's convoluted sentences—is the criticism of his style: " 'Tis dated from the Tower-guard, as a present to his colonel, that his colonel might think him even in time of duty a very contemplative soldier, and I suppose by the roughness of the stile, he writ it there on the butt-end of a musquet."[7] Swift would advance similar objections to Steele's style some twelve years later.

In 1714 Steele himself offered personal insights into the writing of *The Christian Hero* in his *Apology for Himself and his Writings, Occasioned by his Expulsion from the House of Commons.* His confessional tone prodded later critics to assume that Steele was more debauched than he admitted; and he admitted a good deal.

He [Steele] first became an author when an Ensign of the Guards, a way of life exposed to much irregularity; and being thoroughly convinced of many things, of which he often repented, and which he more often repeated, he wrote, for his own private use, a little book called *The Christian Hero,* with a design principally to fix upon his own mind a strong impression of virtue and religion, in opposition to a stronger propensity towards unwarrantable pleasures. This secret admonition was too weak; he therefore printed the book with his name, in hopes that a standing testimony against himself, and the eyes of the world (that is to say of his acquaintance) upon him in a new light, might curb his desires, and make him ashamed of understanding and seeming to feel what was virtuous, and living so quite contrary a life.[8]

Steele's admission of a propensity toward unwarrantable pleasures should not surprise us; he had at least one illegitimate child, and he always acknowledged his wayward fancies. More to the point, however, was his willingness to adopt Elizabeth Ousley, his daughter out of wedlock. He practiced the charity he preached in *The Christian Hero*.

One reader who admired *The Christian Hero* extravagantly was Samuel Keimer, the eccentric printer who employed Benjamin Franklin. In amusing doggerel Keimer says: "Read Richard Steele's bright *Christian Hero*, / I thought that tract might e'en convince a Nero."[9] In 1725 Keimer published Steele's *Crisis,* the first American edition of Steele's work. "His reprinting of a work by Steele [may stem from] the influence he asserts the *Christian Hero* had had in shaping his life."[10]

Later criticism appears to have ignored the book and concentrated upon the author, often with biased dissatisfaction. Friedrich Christoph Schlosser's *History of the Eighteenth Century,* for example, ignorantly misrepresents both the title and genre of Steele's work: "Steele began his career as a writer, with a poem, his *Christian Heroes,* which justified no great expectations. This poem could have little of soul or nature in it, because the contents stood in a most surprising contradiction with Steele's scandalous and dissolute course of life."[11] The tone does not improve much with William Makepeace Thackeray, who rejects the very idea of Steele, the drunkard, writing an ardent devotional work. "Whilst writing this ardent devotional work, he was deep in debt, in drink, and in all the follies of the town; it is related that all the officers of Lucas's, and the gentlemen of the Guards, laughed at Dick. And in truth a theologian in liquor is not a respectable object."[12] Thackeray's tag, "a theologian in liquor," more witty than accurate, remained attached to Steele's literary reputation for the remainder of the nineteenth century.

Such irresponsible criticism continued through the century. Donald Mitchell, for example, dismisses Steele as a fun-loving trooper: ". . . One would hardly have looked to him for any early talk about the life of a true *Christian Hero*. But he did write a book so entitled, in those wild young days, as a sort of kedge anchor, he says, whereby he might haul out from the shoals of the wicked town, and indulge in a sort of contemplative piety. It was and is a very good little book; but it did not hold a bit, as an anchor."[13] Mitchell's witty and sardonic conclusion—the book may be good, but that is irrelevant because Steele was a rake—reveals more about Mitchell than about Steele. A less biased critic is Austin Dobson, who perceived the misreading that Steele's *Apology* was given. Noting that Steele's admission of moral laxity had been expanded by unfriendly critics into fundamental degradation, Dobson, in contrast, suggests that Steele be taken at his word, without embellishment:

It is one of the misfortunes of candour to be always suspected, by those who are not candid, of withholding more than it concedes. Accordingly, the writer of the memoir of Steele in the *Biographia Britannica,* taking this sentence as his authority, expands it thus:—"He spared not to indulge his genius in the wildest excesses, prostituting the exquisite charms of his conversation—talents to give his pleasures a daintier and more poignant relish,"—that is to say, he transforms the author of *The Christian Hero* from an erring and repentant man, conscious of his own stumblings and failings, into a venal and calculating debauchee.[14]

The decline in Steele's reputation has been arrested in the twentieth century, which has taken a more constructive attitude toward his pious tract. The change is attributable largely to Professor Rae Blanchard, whose edition of *The Christian Hero,* published in 1932, reopened scholarly inquiry into Steele's work.[15] Her evaluation is eminently reasonable: *The Christian Hero* "is interesting because it contains the initial expression of some of the ideas—for example, the defense of women and the denunciation of false honour and duelling—which he elaborated in his periodicals, and because his moral theory, his starting-point for two decades of corrective propaganda, is first outlined here."[16]

Chapter Two

Moderate Success in the Theater: *The Funeral, The Lying Lover,* and *The Tender Husband*

The Funeral

Steele's first play, *The Funeral,* was produced at the Drury Lane Theatre late in 1701. Apparently, it was a great success, as Steele himself reports in his *Apology:* "Nothing can make the Town so fond of a Man as a successful Play. . . ."[1] He had written *The Funeral* to revive his reputation after the cool reception of *The Christian Hero,* and it brought him the notice of the king as well as the town. The satire on undertakers appeared as an original stroke, and the satire on lawyers, though not original, suited the taste of the town. The favorable response of the audience continued for many years: "Of Steele's three early plays, *The Funeral* was most frequently performed over a seventy-five-year span."[2]

In the Prologue Steele laughs at his "unnatural" choice of a funeral as a subject for comedy, but of course *The Funeral* has no real funeral at all. The main character, Lord Brumpton, has suffered a temporarily disabling "lethargick-slumber," and only Trusty, his long-time servant, knows that Lord Brumpton is not dead. Meanwhile, Brumpton's young wife—widow, she would like to say—is celebrating her release from the ties of marriage with all the pomp of a funeral ceremony. Brumpton observes her behavior, recognizes her malevolent nature, and dismisses her, but only after he finds her to be a bigamist, married previously to her lover Cabinet. The play, then, depicts a slumber and a moral reawakening; after this experience Lord Brumpton perceives, as he was unable to do before, good and evil as separate and distinct. He sees the virtue of the two couples of the younger generation, Campley and Harriot, Lord Hardy and Sharlot. The play concludes with a change in Brumpton's will, thus ensuring the prosperity of Lord Hardy and a grand call for support of King William, the English army, and Britannia against the French.

Didacticism in *The Funeral*. In a valuable article, Elvena Green summarizes three aspects of Steele's dramatic theory: "(1) that the theatre has a moral, didactic purpose; (2) that in order to fulfill its purpose, the theatre must show innocent, virtuous characters instead of the vicious, licentious ones of the Restoration; (3) that as a result of the substitution of the virtuous characters for wicked ones, the comedy of ridicule and laughter is replaced by a comedy of pity and tears."[3] Professor Green emphasizes Steele's didactic aims in all of his comedies, and rightly so. Steele wants to teach as well as to please.

As a result, most of the characters in *The Funeral* exemplify positive traits worthy of imitation. The most important characters are the gay couple, Campley and Harriot, and the serious couple, Lord Hardy and Sharlot. Superficially they resemble the gay and serious couples of Restoration comedy as they demonstrate opposing attitudes toward love. The gay couple of Steele, however, is by no means like the gay couple of Sir George Etherege; Campley, in fact, resembles Young Bellair rather than Dorimant.

Characterization. In Etherege's *The Man of Mode,* deplored by Steele in *Spectator* 65 and 75, the gay couple of Dorimant and Harriet with their cynical wit held precedence over all other couples; young Bellair and Emilia, the serious couple who love with less wit and more feeling, are subordinated to Dorimant and Harriet. Steele in *The Funeral* has reversed these priorities, giving his serious couple, Lord Hardy and Sharlot, precedence over his gay and witty couple, Campley and Harriot. This shift is significant, for it is feeling and not wit that Steele proposes as the basis of love. Yet even Campley, lively and playful as he is, expresses deep emotion, both in his love for Harriot and his friendship for Hardy; looking forward to the joys of his wedding night is as close as Campley ever comes to the rakishness of Dorimant (a considerable distance, indeed!) and even for this he is rebuked by Lord Hardy.

Steele's gay and serious couples are differentiated more by external manners than by attitudes and beliefs. The serious couple, shy and chaste, are satirized gently for their inability to talk to each other in anything more eloquent than a stutter. Nevertheless, they are the moral leaders to whom the gay couple submit. Harriot's toying with suitors and admiration of her own beauty, though done with wit and flair, are seen as faults, and Sharlot chastises her:

Lady Sharlot: Indeed Sister to be Serious with you, this Vanity in your Humour does not at all become you!

Lady Harriot: Vanity! all the Matter is we Gay People are more sincere than you wise Folks: All your Life's an Art—Speak your Soul—Look you there—Are you not Struck with a Secret Pleasure, when you view that Bloom in your Looks, that Harmony in your Shape, that Promptitude of your Mien!

Lady Sharlot: Well Simpleton, if I am, at First so Silly, as to be a little taken with my self, I know it a Fault, and take pains to correct it. (48)

Harriot accepts this admonition in good humor and later, after Campley makes a similar plea, comes to agree with her sister: "Why should I not obey Reason as soon as I see it?" (52) This reason, which she obeys, arises indeed from Christian ethics—it is a perception of moral duties, an awareness of the moral ruin resulting from pride. Such an understanding of moral duties stems naturally from Steele's *The Christian Hero* and pervades gay and serious couples alike. At the play's conclusion the differences between each couple's manners and language have been removed, and both couples are brought together in opposition to the evil in the "widow" Brumpton.

Steele's character Trusty also expresses his virtue, honesty, good nature, benevolence, and beneficence through feelings as well as actions. Trusty's tears (act 4, sc. 3) are a moral emblem, an indubitable sign of his goodness and veracity. He visits the impoverished Lord Hardy, alienated from his father by the machinations of the new Lady Brumpton, and recounts in mawkish detail his memories of Lord Hardy's mother, his caring for the youthful Lord Hardy, and the last words of Hardy's mother upon her deathbed. While all of this detail may be simply unpleasant to a modern audience, it was a signal to the audience in 1701 that Trusty was trustworthy, that his first interest was justice for the virtuous characters, and that benevolence in his heart would become beneficence in his actions.

Aside from Trusty, who has the character of a servant in name only, Steele began a process, to be completed in *The Conscious Lovers,* of demoting wit and humor to secondary characters, often to servants. Trim, Lord Hardy's personal servant who fancies himself a leader of valiant soldiers, is himself a target of satire, although his master, a pattern of gentility, treats him with kindness in spite of his absurdities. Fate will not be so kind, however, as it allows Trim to profess love and marriage to Mademoiselle D'Epingle, the butt of Steele's satire on French manners. In *The Funeral,* as in other contemporary plays, a sniping at French mannerisms took on the virtue of chauvinistic propaganda, and indeed Steele makes overtly clear his support of war with France at the end of the play. In developing Mademoiselle D'Epingle's character, he mocks female affectation, concern for dress over morality, anxiety to catch a husband, and false appearances. But nothing she does is very serious, and thus, unlike Trim, she is an object of good-natured and tolerant laughter.

Steele's Satire on Undertakers.   Steele launches his satire on funeral undertakers in the Preface to *The Funeral* and continues it as the play begins. After quoting an advertisement for the art of embalming, Steele comments: "He must needs be strangely in Love with this Life, who is not touch'd with this Kind Invitation to be Pickled" (20). But his satire and his anger are not directed against embalming *per se,* but against the abuses and hypocrisy of some of the undertaking brethren. Sable, the undertaker in *The Funeral,* acknowledges hypocrisy as simply a tool of his trade: "The poor Dead are deliver'd to my Custody . . .

not to do them Honour, but to satisfy the Vanity or Interest of their Survivors" (25). Through his employees Sable is a grave-robber and a supplier of mourners, and by himself he is an extortionist in his outrageous demand for a full fee to keep Brumpton's secret. His regular fees are exorbitant. In addition, he acknowledges an alliance with unethical physicians: "Dr. Passeport with the Powder has promised me Six or Seven Funeralls this week" (28).

Steele's concern with social ills and abuses is ably demonstrated in an article by Robert A. Aubin sketching the development of funeral procedures in England before Steele's play. According to Aubin, Steele exposes the following practices, most of them "amply supported by contemporary evidence": ". . . extravagant claims for the efficaciousness of embalming methods, lavishing of funeral honors upon the unworthy, substitution of cheap embalming materials for what had been promised, invention of heraldic devices, orders to hireling mourners to assume 'sad looks,' collusion of undertakers with sextons and others, employment of prostitutes to serve as mourners, and seeking of intelligence of recent deaths."[4] Steele's satire in *The Funeral,* however, extends well beyond undertakers to include rejoicing widows, ragged soldiers, imitative servants, and, especially, dishonest lawyers.

Steele's Satiric Attack Upon Lawyers, or the Use of Language to Prevent Communication. Steele's attack on lawyers (act 1, sc. 2) immediately follows his attack on undertakers, and his anger arises from similar causes: both used their positions to defraud unsuspecting people. In *The Funeral* the lawyer Puzzle visits the apparently distraught young "widow," Lady Brumpton, with the will prepared by her husband. As he waits for admittance, Puzzle explains to his nephew and heir, Tom, the purpose of the will's incomprehensible language and rejoices over the cheat he has put over on the trusting Lord Brumpton. To Tom he relates the secrets of the trade: a lawyer who is master of tautology is master of his client's wishes and can adjust them for his own profit. Puzzle admits with delight the effect of his gibberish: "Now this Gentleman entirely trusted me, and I made the only use a man of Business can of a Trust, I cheated Him;

for I, imperceptibly, before his Face made his whole Estate liable to an Hundred per Annum for my self " (35). The Puzzle instructs Tom not only in writing but also in reading: writing in totally mysterious and incomprehensible tautology and reading in a "Ridiculous Law-Tone" to reinforce the non-meaning. A will that is not understandable provides Puzzle with an excellent opportunity for interpreting it to his advantage.

The upshot of this scene is the rapt wonder of Lord Brumpton and the justified anger of Trusty as they step forth from concealment after having observed the entire proceeding. Their anger ends in frustration—"Oh! that Damn'd Tautologist too—That Puzzle and his Irrevocable Deed!" says Lord Brumpton—and it is only the extraordinary discovery at the conclusion of the play of Lady Brumpton's previous and undissolved marriage to Cabinet before her marriage to Lord Brumpton that causes Puzzle's will to be null and void. It is, in effect, only a mistake by the vicious Cabinet and Lady Brumpton that brings relief from the machinations of the lawyer Puzzle. Evil is only avoided, not defeated. The virtuous Lord Brumpton and Trusty remain powerless against this master of tautology, and at the end Puzzle walks off untouched by retribution and able to continue his vicious ways.

Poor But Honest Soldiers. Steele was a soldier, and, like Lord Hardy of the play, he was to recruit his own men. In addition, England was preparing for war, since Louis XIV of France had "aggravated a bad situation by meddling with the English succession, declaring on the death of James II in September, 1701, that he recognized James's Catholic son as King of England."[5] The likelihood of war must have been a common topic of conversation in late 1701, and therefore the appearance of soldiers and the reference to war in a theatrical entertainment were probably not unexpected. Steele makes clear in his Prologue that the author is a soldier and prepares the way for further references to soldiers (23).[6] Thus it is no surprise to find a gathering of newly recruited soldiers (act 4, sc. 3) ready for examination by Lord Hardy. The theme of the scene combines lighthearted satire on the language, clothing, and mannerisms of these recruits with praise and sympathy for their good-natured naiveté, innocence, and clumsiness. Lord Hardy exhorts his men generously: "Well Gentlemen do your Business Manfully and nothing shall be too good for you" (78).

This scene encourages Englishmen to give greater concern to their soldiers. At the same time the play depicts officers of the army in a most complimentary fashion: Lord Hardy, courageous, honorable, trustworthy; Campley, generous, warm, and true. Hardy's consistent reverence for his father is but an emblem of this idealized soldier's reverence for his country, and Campley's gift of £300 to Hardy indicates his esteem for his friend and fellow soldier. The rousing exhortation in blank verse by Lord Brumpton at the play's conclusion (act 5, sc. 4) ("You are now, Gentlemen, going into Cares at a Crisis in your Country. . . . My rough Plebeian Britains not yet Slaves . . . be thou Honest, Firm, Impartial") is designed to encourage the audience to remember the soldiers in this play and to improve the lot of the recruit while showing respect for officers. While perhaps not effective, the speech concludes a theme present in the play from Act 2, scene 1, onward—the honor and the difficulty in the life of a soldier, a theme of personal importance in Steele's life.

Exemplary Comedy.   Shirley Strum Kenny, in discussing the nature of Steele's comic formula, notes that "Steele began writing with a heritage of the techniques of Restoration comedy, a knack for comic characterization, a penchant for availing himself of foreign sources, an open ear to Collier's exhortation to embrace morality, and, even more important, a personal bent toward didacticism. . . . He was not an original thinker on moral issues; he advocated reason and good sense, benevolence in one's attitudes and actions, emotion as an intensification of one's better qualities, and moral rectitude under all circumstances."[7] As Professor Kenny also indicates, despite Steele's increased emphasis on didactic purpose, his comedies retain an essential comic aspect. "To enliven morality with wit, and to temper wit with morality" is as applicable to Steele's plays as to the *Tatler* and *Spectator*.

The gay and serious couples, Campley and Harriot, Lord Hardy and Sharlot, exemplify Steele's comic and didactic methods. At the opening of the play both couples diverge from the ideals of courtship. The painful shyness of the serious couple prevents the adequate expression of their thoughts and feelings; the flippant affectation of Harriot and the mild rakishness of Campley, while permitting a match of wits in a love game, prevent communication between the would-be lovers. Both couples progress to a more balanced, more open, and less affected courtship based not on pleasure but on a serious preparation for marriage. Steele evokes laughter at the shy meetings of Hardy and Sharlot and at the antics of Campley and Harriot, and yet he fulfills his didactic purpose by developing both couples into models of young people preparing for marriage.

Sensitivity to the possibility that his audience might imitate some of his characters may have led Steele to be concerned with poetic justice; in any case, poetic justice is distributed to the major characters, so that Cabinet, the villainess Lady Brumpton, and Tattleaid are dismissed while the virtuous characters share the joy of their deliverance. Lord Brumpton calls this group his family, including not only his son but both couples and Trusty. It is Trusty indeed who has expedited the action which leads to the success of good over evil, morality over immorality, in sexual conduct and filial relations. Trusty teaches Lord Brumpton, and by implication the audience, a lesson: to adhere to strict justice and to retain familial ties against the demands of sexual attraction. The "moral lessons" balance the play's wit and sight comedy, making *The Funeral* both a didactic and a comic success.

Hilarious Comedy and Farce. Visual comedy is a strong point in *The Funeral;* there are numerous scenes, some bordering on or even becoming farce, which are hilariously funny and capable of making the most stony-faced break into a smile. Among them are the singing of Mrs. Fardingale (act 2, sc. 3), the change of clothes between Harriot and Mademoiselle D'Epingle, with Campley dressed as a woman (act 3, sc. 3), and the soldiers gathered and ready for the attack on Lord Brumpton's house (act 4, sc. 3; act 5, sc. 2; act 5, sc. 3).[8] The audience laughs at the foibles of a pretender, Mrs. Fardingale squalling as she pretends to sing, Mademoiselle D'Epingle pretending to be a lady, and Trim haranguing his rag-tag soldiers as he pretends to be Alexander leading his army.[9] In these scenes Steele's situational comedy is not overshadowed by his didacticism. *The Funeral* was an excellent first effort at comedy; "the play was successful because it deserved to be."[10]

The Lying Lover

Steele's second play, a comedy entitled *The Lying Lover: or, The Ladies Friendship,* appeared on the stage in 1703 and in print approximately two months later (107). Steele's didactic purpose, evident in *The Funeral,* is more obtrusive in this, his only failure. *The Lying Lover* ran for six nights initially, underwent a revival of four nights in 1746, and then disappeared from the stage. Despite its failure, it offers delightful sight comedy which would probably be enjoyable on the stage today. The problem with the play occurs in the fifth act, in the awkward, unpleasant, and overemphasized repentance of Young Bookwit for the supposed murder of his friend Lovemore. As Steele says, the play was written for the essential moral suasion of the repentance scene.[11]

In the last line of the fifth act Steele presents to the reader/audience the "just maxim" upon which the whole lesson of *The Lying Lover* is built: "There is no gallantry in Love but Truth" (118). Successful human relationships require trust, honesty, and truth; deception and hypocrisy, even when derived from an apparently innocent excess of vanity, only destroy the relationships most sought. Steele illustrates his thesis in three separate, though interrelated, areas of human experience: romantic love, parental and filial affection, and friendship.

The first four acts display various destructive tendencies within a number of relationships: the results of vain lying, tortured jealousy, and hypocritical posturing. Young Bookwit lies in order to appear an urbane, experienced man of the world before Penelope, who is engaged to the jealous Lovemore. Penelope encourages the silly posturing of the sophomoric Bookwit, while exacerbating the jealousy of the man she truly loves. The lying of Young Bookwit causes a breakdown of trust and love between Lovemore and Penelope as well as between Penelope and her best friend, Victoria. It also brings Young Bookwit and his friend

Lovemore to a duel in which the drunken Young Bookwit apparently kills his former friend. Meanwhile, Young Bookwit has been deceiving his father as well, who has trusted implicitly in his son's veracity and goodness. The acts of deception arouse anger and hatred and destroy the trust necessary to marital, parental, and filial love, as well as to friendship. Steele presents a sometimes funny, sometimes stern warning as he illustrates his theme in the first four acts of *The Lying Lover:* "Such deserv'd misfortunes they must share / Who with gay Falsehoods entertain the Fair" (act 5, sc. 3).

    Plot.   The play focuses on Young Bookwit, the lying lover, who with his friend Latine has emerged from the university and recently arrived in London. He wishes to appear the dashing hero, gallant with the ladies and valiant as a soldier, and to this end he concocts monstrous lies about his exploits in battle. Latine agrees to act as his footman in this expedition in the great world. They meet with Penelope and her friend, Victoria, and Young Bookwit engages in a conversation which concludes with his profession of love. Immediately after Young Bookwit falsely and extravagantly informs Lovemore that Penelope was his guest for a collation and entertainment on the water the previous evening. Young Bookwit defends his lying to Latine simply as a means to an instant reputation.

    Unfortunately, Lovemore believes all that Young Bookwit has said, and he berates Penelope for her inconstancy. Instead of speaking to him truthfully, Penelope toys with Lovemore's jealousy, teasing him to a frenzy while allowing him to adhere to his jealous fears. As Lovemore plans his revenge on Young Bookwit, Penelope contrives, with Victoria's help, a secret meeting with Young Bookwit. Meanwhile, Old Bookwit, the old-fashioned, somewhat doddering, but loving and sincere father, reveals his plans for his son's marriage to Penelope, only to be greeted with the most extravagant lies and deception. The credulous old man, duped by his love for his son, believes all and goes to make his apology to Penelope's father.

    Penelope and Victoria secretly visit Latine and Young Bookwit, who unwittingly serenades Penelope in the belief that she is

Victoria, much to the laughter and merriment of the ladies. They mock Young Bookwit's pretensions to military valor as well as gallantry among the ladies. Defeated in his stratagems, Young Bookwit retires to a tavern for refuge and forgetfulness.

Shortly after leaving the tavern, the drunken Young Bookwit meets Lovemore, immediately invites a duel, and Lovemore apparently is killed in the ensuing clash. Young Bookwit, Latine, and Penelope's servant Simon are hauled to prison. Old Bookwit, ever the loving father, is almost distracted with grief; in an emotional scene he appeals to Lovemore's friend, Frederick, for help. Meanwhile, Young Bookwit, Latine, and Simon are subjected to the horrors of Newgate Prison, among prisoners who have no future but the gallows.

After a restorative sleep, Young Bookwit awakens in Newgate with memories of his drunken duel with Lovemore and bemoans his wretchedness. Unknown to him, Lovemore's wound is minor and now Frederick disguises Lovemore as a sergeant who may observe unnoticed the reactions of both Young Bookwit and Penelope. The remorse of both Young Bookwit and Penelope and the agony of Old Bookwit soften Lovemore so that he throws off his disguise, embraces Bookwit and Latine in friendship, and offers his love once more to Penelope, who accepts him warmly. Parents, friends, and lovers are reconciled as truth and trust overcome the misunderstandings caused by Young Bookwit's earlier deceptions.

Comedy of Ridicule vs. Exemplary Comedy. Steele planned a radical deviation from the rules of comedy and even from the practice of most Restoration comedies as he constructed *The Lying Lover;* perhaps he took the challenge from Jeremy Collier's strictures on the English stage and saw himself forging a new kind of instructive comedy based on imitation, not ridicule. In any case, he announced the moral basis of his new play in the Preface: "I thought therefore it would be an honest Ambition to attempt a Comedy, which might be no improper Entertainment in a Christian Commonwealth" (115). Although the first four acts of *The Lying Lover* are free from "improper" references to church, deity, or morality, Steele's reforming instinct is truly revealed

in the fifth act, where through the power of pious emotion—
called by Steele Anguish and Sorrow—an erring character repents
and turns his life from vice to virtue. The depiction of anguish
and sorrow and their effects, asserts Steele, "are, perhaps, an
Injury to the Rules of Comedy, but I am sure they are a Justice
to those of Morality" (115). Not only does Young Bookwit reject
his vanity and lying, but Penelope and Lovemore, in the midst
of intense emotional stress, undergo reformation as well, by overcoming jealousy and abandoning coquettish teasing. The lengthy
emotional reformation scenes transform *The Lying Lover* into a
comedy of tears.

In his *Apology* Steele credits Jeremy Collier with his inspiration
to write a severely moral, in this case lachrymose, comedy. He
was, he says, "a great Admirer of [Collier's] work, and took it
into [his] Head to write a Comedy in the Severity he required"
(*Ap,* 311). He goes on somewhat defensively and disingenuously
to blame the poor reception of his play on its morality rather than
on its inherent weaknesses of structure, plot, and characterization:
"Considering me as a Comick Poet, I have been a Martyr and
Confessor for the Church; for this play was damn'd for its Piety"
(*Ap,* 312). Be that as it may, Steele's *Apology* offers another source
for his new kind of comedy; it is no accident that the paragraphs
preceding his discussion of *The Lying Lover* contain quotations
from *The Christian Hero.* The ideas on ethics and epistemology
that he presented in *The Christian Hero* provide the rationale for
the repentance and reformation in the fifth act of *The Lying Lover.*

In *The Christian Hero* Steele suggests that religion must be
enlisted as an aid to reason in order effectively to guide the
passions, the motivators of human action, to virtuous conduct.
Young Bookwit demonstrates the inadequacy of reason alone as
a guide to virtue; all of Latine's expostulations are ineffectual
against the vanity and pride of his friend. After he awakens in
prison, Young Bookwit recognizes the inadequacy of his reason
to effect a change in his life; throughout his discussion with
Latine he stresses the weakness of reason while pleading for grace
from heaven. Though he appears to be in despair, he still calls
to heaven for help: "But nothing mix with this celestial Drop, /

But Dew from that high Heav'n of which 'tis part" (175). The celestial Drop is Young Bookwit's soul, and the Dew, of course, is divine grace. Latine offers him a benediction: "May that high Heav'n compose your Mind / And reconcile you to yourself." In this central scene (act 5, sc. 1), reason, proven ineffectual as a moral guide, is now joined by religion and grace to gain control of the passions; the result is repentance for past actions and a veritable and drastic adjustment in the direction and control of future ethical conduct. [12] Young Bookwit's penitential scene presents the moral of the play both in precept and action. [13]

Although Steele may have broken new ground with this play, much of the sight comedy of the first four acts derives from the well-tried methods of the comedy of ridicule. The fifth act, in contrast, belongs completely to the comedy of imitation, or exemplary comedy, in which characters exemplify ideals of conduct and behavior for imitation by the audience. The disparity in dramatic methodologies causes a dysfunction in plot structure and in characterization between the fourth and fifth acts which in turn causes the play's failure. *The Lying Lover* may be identified as a transitional exemplary comedy, with potentially ideal characters—Young Bookwit, Penelope, and Lovemore—who become exemplary through their penitential experiences in the fifth act. When Steele developed the exemplary model fully for his comic drama and substituted scenes of recognition for scenes of penitence, as with *The Conscious Lovers,* he achieved success.

Learning to Love and to Trust: Preparing for Marriage. Steele's appreciation of the sermons of Dr. John Tillotson, as well as his respect for the reforms of Jeremy Collier, may have inspired him to try his hand at homiletic comedy, for his lesson on marriage in *The Lying Lover* is both more grave and more idealized than the courtships in *The Funeral.* In his first play Steele was content to subordinate the gay couple and to have them ultimately realize the value of a serious approach to marriage. In *The Lying Lover* Steele's adjustments to the gay couple/serious couple dichotomy often used in Restoration comedy are more thorough and less successful.

As the play opens, the overly serious and jealous Lovemore is engaged to the witty, vivacious Penelope. Her friend, Victoria, though lively, tends to be more reserved and serious. Young Bookwit, the extravagantly artificial and insincere spark about town, contrives to introduce himself by catching Penelope as she almost falls, but thinks her name is Victoria. The gay couple, at this point Penelope and Young Bookwit, cause great anguish and jealousy to both Lovemore, who truly loves Penelope, and Victoria, who discovers her own attraction to Young Bookwit. Their gaiety and wit turn out to be immature, insubstantial, and uncharitable. They are by no means evil, but they show themselves selfish in their disregard for other people. Penelope teases the irascible Lovemore by ignoring him, and Lovemore responds with mistrust and jealous anger. Young Bookwit dallies cavalierly with Penelope, causing strife between her and Lovemore, while he lies outrageously to Lovemore about his assignations with Penelope, all to make himself appear a witty rake in everyone's eyes. His stratagem fails, however, and he discovers through his duel the suffering and danger caused by his deception of Penelope and Lovemore. As selfish and careless personalities all, Young Bookwit, Lovemore, and Penelope become the objects of Steele's satire.

The reformation of all three of the characters in act 5 changes their attitudes substantially. Penelope repents her cruelty to Lovemore with tears and expressions of sincere love, as she hears from Frederick that her husband-to-be is dead. Lovemore, who in a sergeant's disguise hears her professions of love, repents his jealousy; throwing off his sergeant's gown he promises never again to doubt Penelope's faithfulness. Penelope's recognition of her strong love for Lovemore makes her more serious, and Lovemore's newfound trust in her allows him to be less serious and more open. Thus, at the conclusion of *The Lying Lover* Penelope and Lovemore exemplify an ideal reserved couple, both aware of the dangers to their love from coquettish giddiness and distrusting jealousy and both trusting now in the serious and mature nature of their relationship. Young Bookwit changes too, as he undergoes a long, detailed contrition for his faults; after being forgiven by his friend Lovemore and promising to put aside all deceit, the newly serious Young Bookwit receives the reward of his repentance, Victoria. The always honest and serious Victoria will modify and improve the behavior of the penitent, as they pledge their faith and trust to each other: "Victoria: I believe I may safely promise to approve of all the truth he tells me." "Young Bookwit: You've promis'd then to like all I shall say" (187). Both couples, then, confront the duties and responsibilities of marriage seriously, and in so doing become examples for the audience and the reader.

Friendship: Affection, Jealousy, and Renewal. Friendship as well as marriage is a major concern in *The Lying Lover*. Steele depicts friendship as an extraordinary relationship of great value, which can be ruined by carelessness, affectation, or jealousy. Two of the three friendships in this play are disrupted by selfish concerns; all, however, end stronger and more mature than they began.

The most obvious pair of friends in the play are Young Bookwit and Latine, the two undergraduates who pose as master and servant entering the great world. Although Young Bookwit ignores Latine's admonitions throughout his extravagant career in deception, he never lies to him, nor does Latine ever entertain the thought of deceiving his friend. Theirs is a worthy friendship; but the overwhelming evidence of Latine's exemplary dedication to his friendship comes in act 5, where he offers to take responsibility for the supposed death of Lovemore and to die in the place of Young Bookwit. His willingness to give up his life for his friend—the highest manifestation of friendship—is one cause for Lovemore's throwing off his disguise in act 5 and embracing Latine and young Bookwit in restored friendship. The example of Latine's fidelity has the immediate effect upon Lovemore of reconciliation and renewal of friendship, ideals which Steele holds up for his audience.

The friendship between Young Bookwit and Lovemore, so warmly renewed in act 5, is broken earlier by Lovemore's jealousy of Young Bookwit, who has claimed to be a lover of Penelope. Steele appears to have planned this estrangement for the benefit of the duel scene (act 4, sc. 3), wherein the irrational impulses arising from drunkenness and extreme jealousy combine to bring a clash of swords. Young Bookwit, befuddled and unthinking, wishes to take the life of a friend; Steele shows the bestial nature of his attempt and displays the stupidity of dueling for honor. The repentance scene allows Young Bookwit full opportunity to denounce dueling, which he blames on the devil's opposition to the divine law of forgiveness and calls the "damn'd last shift of the damn'd envious Foe of Human Race" (176).

In contrast to the gravity of the male friendships is the delightfully funny opposition of Penelope and Victoria as they become aware of their mutual attraction to Young Bookwit. Their affected concern for one another's beauty and real determination to spoil all that art hath wrought offers "one of the funniest scenes (act 3, sc. 1) Steele ever wrote" (104). The young women treat each other with stiff formality, and in stiffer imitation their maids, Lettice and Betty, attempt the formality of their betters. In mock concern for each other Penelope and Victoria add powder to each other's hair and patches to each other's faces until they look like sprites. Steele's adept use of sight comedy shows the dramatist at his best; one can imagine the audience's laughter (while the women work destructively with patches and powder) as Victoria says, "I have a Patch-box about me. Hold, my dear, that gives you a sedate Air, that large one near your Temples"— and as Penelope replies, "Let me put a little Disdain in your Face . . . There—that on your Forehead does it" (152). Fortunately, both Penelope and Victoria perceive the danger of jealousy to their friendship; and when Lovemore's supposed death brings home to Penelope the superficiality and selfishness of her concerns, it becomes clear that Victoria and Penelope will not again allow jealousy to break their friendship. The lesson is repeatedly urged upon audience and reader.

Father and Son: The Generation Gap Again.   The relationship between Old Bookwit and his prodigal son provides a homily on filial love. Although the ideal of mutual love and respect is temporarily broken by Young Bookwit's selfish deception of his father, in the reconciliation scene both father and son exemplify the ideal of parental and filial love restored and strengthened. It is undeniable that "Steele considered the relations between parents and children of prime importance in his moral scheme."[14]

Steele initially characterizes Old Bookwit as the type of doddering and old-fashioned male familiar to readers of Restoration comedy. His congratulating himself on speaking words of love to Penelope makes him a butt of laughter, not unlike Old Bellair in *The Man of Mode*. His marriage plans for his son, concocted by the two fathers without consulting either son or daughter, reveal his out-of-date attitude about a child's right to refuse a proposed marriage. There the similarity to the stock old man ends, however, for Old Bookwit responds to his son throughout the play not with senile impatience but rather with kindness and warm emotion. Old Bookwit's superficial faults, then, are overshadowed by goodness and love; his relationship with Young Bookwit—a loving father but a selfish son—is a corollary of the relationships—a selfish father but a dutiful son—of Lord Brumpton and Lord Hardy in *The Funeral*. In both plays Steele instructs the audience and the reader in the value of parental and filial love.

The son has much to atone for in his repentance. Old Bookwit's cry, as he swoons, "Oh Child! you've broke your Father's Heart," brings a response from Young Bookwit—"Yet if my Sighs, my Tears, my Anguish can atone"—which reconciles father and son (183–84). Other characters are off stage during this scene, so that the entire attention of the audience focuses on the pathos of the emotion and suffering.

Steele took a typecast old man and changed him into Old Bookwit for his didactic purposes, unfortunately with only partial success. The pathos is overwhelming and without relief. With considerable modification under Steele's hand this character becomes, over time, the more successful Sir John Bevil, and Young Bookwit of the fifth act, dutiful and warmly responsive to his father, becomes Bevil, Jr., in *The Conscious Lovers*.

The Tender Husband

Steele's third play, *The Tender Husband,* contrasts markedly with his two earlier comedies. If one were hoping to find continued and perhaps expected progress toward a fully developed exemplary comedy, then *The Tender Husband* would be a disappointment, for Steele has reverted to the methods of comedy of ridicule. In fact, there is little evidence of exemplary comedy anywhere about it.[15] Nevertheless, *The Tender Husband* was not only well received upon its appearance in April and May, 1705, but it is generally regarded, with *The Conscious Lovers,* as one of Steele's two best plays. A laughing comedy, it is filled with witty satire, and it became a staple of the repertory for most of the next forty years. Feeling a measure of contentment with the success of his latest production, Steele dedicated his play to his friend Joseph Addison as a "memorial of an inviolable friendship." In his Dedication Steele proclaimed the decency and high moral tone of *The Tender Husband:* "I should not offer it to you as such had I not been very careful to avoid everything that might look ill-natured, immoral, or prejudicial to what the better part of mankind hold sacred and honorable" (209). Despite this prudent tone Steele does not aim to instruct the audience through exemplary characters or even through didactic language; the instructive element, extraordinarily mild, is presented at the conclusion of the play in three couplets: "You've seen th' extreams of the Domestick Life / A Son too much confin'd—too free a Wife; / By generous bonds you either should restrain / And only on their Inclinations gain, / Wives to Obey must Love, Children revere / While only Slaves are govern'd by their fear." As Steele suggests in the first couplet, he presents lessons in how not to live, in how not to treat a wife, a son, or a daughter; he has returned to the traditional rules of comedy by depicting and satirizing the errors and foibles of his characters.[16]

Plot.   Steele constructed *The Tender Husband* with a dual plot. The title refers to Clerimont, Sr., and his attempt to cure his wife of the fashionable vices instigated by a tour of France. In this half of the play Clerimont, Sr., persuades his former mistress, Lucy, to masquerade as a pretty gentleman named Fairlove and to profess love to Mrs. Clerimont. Clerimont, Sr., claims that he desires to reform his wife or to cast her off, depending upon the evidence of her virtue, and he allows Lucy to play her part hoping she can replace Mrs. Clerimont as his wife. His indiscreet wife writes a letter inviting Fairlove to visit her late at night; Fairlove gives the letter to Clerimont, Sr., and together they go to the assignation, with the husband hiding until a moment opportune for surprise. He springs forward, drawing his sword and catching his wife in the plot he himself has concocted with Fairlove. She swoons upon seeing the letter, but revives with anger as she hears that Fairlove is indeed a woman and her husband's mistress. Although Clerimont, Sr., appears the stern judge, threatening his wife with his sword as she prays for mercy, his heart melts as she professes penitence. He forgives her, claims to have reformed her, and insists that she shed her foppery by degrees.

Until the very night that the play opened, the title was different.[17] Called "The City Nymph" after Biddy Tipkin, this title referred to the other plot, the courtship of a wealthy young woman, Biddy Tipkin, by an impecunious younger brother, Captain Clerimont. Reacting to the grossly money-minded attitudes of her guardians, Hezekiah and Barsheba Tipkin, Biddy immerses herself in a world of heroic romances and enjoys dreaming of the trials and tribulations of a long-thwarted, gallant love. Her guardians attempt to force her to marry her country bumpkin cousin, Humphry Gubbin, who, it turns out, hates her as much as she hates him. Together they conspire to deceive his father and her guardians. Meanwhile, the poor younger brother of Clerimont, Sr., Captain Clerimont, who is conversant also with the French romances, woos Biddy as Parthenissa in the artificial language and manner she has adopted. Although Humphry leads Biddy to the church, the gallant Captain Clerimont marries her; Humphry, who has come to town to marry and does not wish to return home empty-handed, naively accepts the necessitous Lucy, Clerimont, Sr.'s discarded mistress. The character who links the two plots together is Samuel Pounce, lawyer for the Tipkins and the Gubbins and brother to Lucy. Pounce knows all secrets and for-

wards the action as an offer of one thousand pounds from Clerimont, Sr., and his own interest dictate. Pounce epitomizes the
genial self-interest that all of the characters obey.

Good Humor in the Comedy of Ridicule. Steele follows
a middle course as he delineates his characters in *The Tender
Husband,* for, while there is not a single exemplary character to
be found in the play, the faults each displays are foibles, weaknesses, or eccentricities rather than vices or evils. As a result,
these characters are satirized amusingly, not solemnly. In fact,
the satire is distinctly Horatian, genial laughter at the faults held
up to view. Despite the jibe at lawyers and the mockery of
Barsheba Tipkin's love of stocks and bonds, the "values of the
play . . . reveal no distinct hostility to the merchants. The two
social groups (gentry and merchant) are clearly defined and their
rivalry is central to the play; yet there is no suggestion, through
satire, that they should remain apart."[18] The satire, then, is
directed generally against personal eccentricities, and the values
promulgated through the satire are good nature and generosity.

The most serious display of ill nature and foolishness occurs
in the primary plot between Clerimont, Sr., and Mrs. Clerimont.
Although Mrs. Clerimont reveals in her foppery a forgetfulness
of sound English values, she is still, as her husband says, true
to his bed though careless of his fortune. In contrast, Clerimont,
Sr., shows in his plotting with his mistress against his wife a
hard-heartedness more worthy of condemnation than any weakness in her character. Critics disagree about the effect of the
reconciliation in the fifth act, one suggesting that indeed Mrs.
Clerimont has been retrieved from her erring ways by her firm
but patient husband and another suggesting that Mrs. Clerimont
dupes Clerimont, Sr., by appealing to his vanity and desire for
control.[19] In any case, Clerimont, Sr.'s desire to preserve appearances, which is never cured, and Mrs. Clerimont's extravagant
vanity in wishing to be the toast of the town are major weaknesses
inviting derision and laughter from the audience and reader.

Eliciting less antipathy and more genial laughter than the
Clerimonts is Biddy Tipkin, whom John Loftis calls "the most
charming of Steele's female characters."[20] Biddy refuses to accept

the values of shopkeepers as her own; she refuses indeed to accept her aunt's definition of the comfortable life, which is "to live with prudence and frugality, as we do in Lombard Street." Instead, Biddy has replaced this with the vicarious experience of love and honor in heroic romance. She even changes her name to Parthenissa, one of the heroines of upper-class romance. Both the narrow-minded avarice of the aunt and the day-dreaming imagination of the niece deserve laughter; yet the values of the heroic romances are not wholly cast away. Captain Clerimont is knowledgeable in the romances too, and this common preference suggests a potentially harmonious marriage. The values of love and honor promulgated in the French heroic romances and in Dryden's heroic drama are by no means unworthy of serious consideration, and, shorn of extravagance, these works promote a code for living in an amoral world which is not unlike Biddy's situation.[21] Captain Clerimont, though enriching himself through marriage, is still a positive character, saving Biddy from the tyranny of Lombard Street and to some degree making real Biddy's dreams founded in heroic romance.

In stark contrast to Biddy and her successful dreams are Samuel Pounce, who has no dreams and no illusions, and his sister Lucy, whose dreams of love give way to a marriage of convenience. Pounce is a manipulator, a knave in a world of fools and knaves, a mildly fearful figure who manages all sorts of people with appeals to vanity or hypocrisy. Yet the ends which his amoral machinations effect in this play are generally positive, and thus Pounce escapes severe censure. Lawyer Pounce simply services the needs of others, whatsoever they be, in a most effective, practical, and, of course, profitable fashion. "The Pounces are a family that will always have money," says Pounce to Sir Harry at play's end; such worldly success evokes the audience's—and probably Steele's too in 1705—grudging admiration. The same kind of unsinkable sturdiness appears in Pounce's sister, Lucy, who, though she loses a lover, makes the best of a bad situation and gains a financially favorable marriage (*TH,* xviii). Though no one envies her marriage to Humphry, she does well in a world of deception and intrigue, perhaps even gaining a better situation than Mrs. Clerimont's.

Marriage: For Love or Money?   The choice of a marriage partner was in Steele's day, as it is still today, a decision of unparalleled significance. In eighteenth-century England potential marriage partners were not inhibited from seeking a comfortable financial settlement as the basis for a successful marriage. For many people in Steele's day the most promising marriage required financial security as well as mutual love. Less than ideal—and perhaps more common—marriages required sufficient financial resources to ensure a respectable station, and from this comfort mutual esteem might arise. Marriages for love alone, ignoring the need for money, were seen by the prudent as doomed to failure. The pre-eminent importance of money in marriage informs all of the spouse-seeking in *The Tender Husband.*

Biddy Tipkin and Captain Clerimont have both read French heroic romances, but Clerimont knows also that money is essential for their happiness. Such a clear-eyed, worldly attitude on the part of this younger brother fortune-hunter does not make him a villain. Indeed, his attitude only suggests an experience of a world far removed from heroic romance such as Biddy, like Lydia Languish in Sheridan's *The Rivals,* has not yet acquired. The primary purpose of their courtship, from Clerimont's perspective, is to ensure a financially satisfying life and, from Biddy's, to escape from the tyranny of her guardians. Their mutual attraction is an added benefit, perhaps pointing to a "most promising" marriage.

Essentially the same motivation (a desire for financial security) that attracts Captain Clerimont to Biddy also directs Lucy to Humphry Gubbin. Humphry and Lucy are distinctly different, however, in that both are flawed by past experience, the country bumpkin by his boorish upbringing under a domineering father and the castoff mistress by her liaison with Clerimont, Sr. Yet each fulfills the need of the other, since Gubbin wants to return home with a wife—any wife—and Lucy needs the financial security of a marriage contract. The audience understands that this is not an ideal marriage, but then theirs is not an ideal world. Neither Gubbin nor Lucy enters marriage with illusions of love, and yet the financial security in the contract may well make theirs a successful marriage, if only on the level of practicality and self-interest.[22]

Tyrannical Father and Rebellious Son. Both Sir Harry Gubbin and his son Humphry furnish amusing material for Steele's satire, but he treats Humphry with tolerance and Sir Harry with disdain. For that matter, Humphry is portrayed sympathetically as the down-trodden and oppressed, yet still spirited son of a tyrannical father. Sir Harry, on the other hand, is severely censured as an unfeeling father. His opening line, "Look y', Brother Tipkin, as I told you before, my Business in Town is to dispose of an Hundred Head of Cattle, and my Son," expresses his disposition toward his son: Humphry is no more than property to Sir Harry, an object among his other wealth (225). Steele had always expressed his firm disapproval of oppression of the weak and disenfranchised, whether on the personal or political level. As in all of his other plays, he analyzes the paternal/filial relationship; whereas in *The Lying Lover* the relationship between Young Bookwit and his father is retrieved from ruin in the fifth act, the relationship between Sir Harry and Humphry, if it may be called that, is irretrievable. By the very nature of the comedy, based on the ridicule of faults and eccentricities, the father and son in *The Tender Husband* depict what not to be and do. The fault is primarily Sir Harry's, who governs a son by fear and deception instead of by love.[23]

As a result, Humphry receives the audience's sympathy, especially as he uses his wits to trick his father and achieve independence. John Loftis describes Humphry as "the most attractive of the stage bumpkins of the time."[24] This may be partially a result of Steele's emphasizing the appealing qualities of his younger characters and the stodgy, selfish qualities of his oldsters, who appear as obstacles to the happiness of the younger generation. Humphry's attractiveness may also arise from his throwing off the oppression of a father who has lost his right to authority by his misgovernment. In any case, Humphry became the inspiration for other sympathetically portrayed country bumpkins, most notably, of course, Tony Lumpkin of *She Stoops to Conquer*.[25]

The Francophile Ridiculed.   In the early years of the eighteenth century almost any mention of French manners on the
English stage was sure to elicit a strong reaction from the audience. The War of the Spanish Succession heightened a tradition
of francophobia, and an English audience in 1705 would have
appreciated the delicious ridicule of an Englishwoman who aban-
doned virtuous old English ways for foppish, modern French
manners. Clerimont, Sr.'s wife could never enjoy audience sympathy. Her delight with French customs, apparently including
indiscreet flirtations, is linked in the mind of the English audience
with an abandonment of the ways of virtue, though her delight
with things French and her affair with Fairlove could be independent. Even Clerimont, Sr., sees her errors arising from her
travels through France, "where she learn'd to lose her Money
Gracefully, to admire every Vanity in our Sex, and contemn every
Virtue in her own" (218). The anti-French theme is reinforced
by the reference to the Duke of Marlborough's success—"the
General makes such hast to finish the War, that we Red-coats
may be soon out of Fashion"—and by the appealing qualities of
Captain Clerimont, a soldier with urbanity and wit.

The errors resulting from Mrs. Clerimont's imitation of the
French lead to her ambiguous repentance scene (act 5, sc. 1) with
Clerimont, Sr., in which she apparently renounces her erring
ways because of her respect for her husband, who appears brutish
and unworthy of her respect. A possible explanation for the seeming confusion is the addition of a section in the fifth act by
Addison, who perhaps had not adequately adapted his lines to
Steele's characters.[26] For example, dueling, which Steele detested,
is oddly used to persuade Mrs. Clerimont of her duty. Addison's
contribution may have altered the characterization sufficiently so
that the repentance becomes awkward.

There is, indeed, a gulf between *The Tender Husband* and Steele's
last play, *The Conscious Lovers*. Whereas *The Tender Husband* is a
restrained comedy of ridicule, *The Conscious Lovers* is Steele's most
fully developed rendering of an exemplary comedy, and the model
for exemplary comedy during much of the eighteenth century.

Chapter Three

Success in Exemplary Comedy: *The Conscious Lovers*

The Conscious Lovers

In *The Conscious Lovers,* his last and best play, Steele adhered totally to his theory of exemplary comedy by offering for the audience's imitation both male and female ideals of behavior. It should be no surprise that Steele's new comedy elicited sharply critical responses from literary theorists, such as John Dennis, who held to the classical theory of comedy. Nevertheless, Steele attempted to justify his exemplary comedy by the authority of the Roman dramatist Terence.

The Conscious Lovers is an adaptation of Terence's *Andria,* but plot, characterization, and tone are changed drastically after act 1, scene 1, by Steele's emphasis upon benevolent precept and example. Indeed, Steele calls his play "a translation" of Terence in his Preface, but unquestionably the theme of *The Conscious Lovers* is Steele's, the same theme of moral instruction which fills the pages of *The Christian Hero* as well as the *Tatler* and the *Spectator.* Steele may well have read Terence in light of his own sensibilities, for in *Spectator 502* he presented as a motto for Christian benevolence a quotation from Terence's *Heautontimo-rumenos: homo sum: humani nil a me alienum puto.*[1] Some readers look upon Steele's rendering of this line as "sensibility for all mankind" as a purposeful misrepresentation, while others suggest that Steele simply misinterpreted Terence. In any case Steele saw in Terence a classical writer who apparently developed in his comedies the sensibility of which Steele approved. By claiming Terence as his authority Steele found a precedent for his theory of exemplary comedy, though in fact *The Conscious Lovers* is a far cry from Terence's *Andria.*

John Dennis argued strenuously against Steele's exemplary comedy, but theater-goers disagreed.[2] *The Conscious Lovers* was a conspicuous success. "During its first season it brought in £2,536 3s 6d, more money than any play previously performed by the company."[3] Yet the play had been slow in maturing, although the appearance of *The Conscious Lovers* at Drury Lane, almost two decades after *The Tender Husband,* should not lead one to the impression that Steele had forgotten the drama during this time. Nor had his ideas about the purpose and value of the theater changed. In fact, Steele had probably been working on his play for ten to twelve years, since the days of the *Tatler* and the *Spectator.* It is mentioned, from time to time, as "The Fine Gentleman," or "The Gentleman," or "The Unfashionable Gentleman," and usually as a play about to be finished. Steele, of course, had his debts to prod him to finish his play, or at least to suggest its near completion. Although he probably did not realize it at the time, the arguments that he used against *The Man Of Mode* in *Spectator* 65 serve well as arguments for the exemplary characters in *The Conscious Lovers.* Steele believed that an audience is encouraged to imitate indiscriminately the characters appearing on a stage, whether they are Dorimant and Sir Fopling Flutter or Bevil, Jr., and Charles Myrtle. It is not surprising then that he would find Dorimant dangerous, as did Jeremy Collier; it is only reasonable that he would attempt to replace Dorimant with Bevil, Jr. But whether any young man ever left the theater determined to imitate Bevil, Jr.,—or even Charles Myrtle—is at best debatable.

Steele had presented some of the characters in *The Conscious Lovers* three years earlier, in his last periodical, the *Theatre.*[4] Purportedly written by Sir John Edgar, who becomes Sir John Bevil in the play, the *Theatre* begins with a gallery of characters interested in the British theater; their discussions lead to a defense of the quality of drama at Drury Lane, whose patent and license Steele had held since 1715. Much of *The Conscious Lovers* must have been written by 1720, for Steele draws on his play for incident and character in the *Theatre*. He even refers to the quarrel between Bevil, Jr., and Myrtle in *Theatre 19*, but places it in the third act instead of the fourth. This evidence suggests that *The Conscious Lovers* was written before 1720, but that Steele revised it before its appearance on the stage in 1722. The characters from *The Conscious Lovers* provide one of the few light and pleasant touches to a journal otherwise devoted to a bitter struggle with the Duke of Newcastle over the exercise of the Drury Lane patent and to a discussion of finances involving the South Sea Company. Unfortunately, the potential for developing Sir John Edgar and company is not realized in the *Theatre*'s twenty-eight fragmented and argumentative issues. Sir John's characters had to wait for *The Conscious Lovers* and the stage at Drury Lane in 1722.

Plot. *The Conscious Lovers* opens with a dialogue between Sir John Bevil and his old servant, Humphrey, about the impending marriage of Bevil, Jr., and Lucinda Sealand, daughter of a wealthy London merchant. Humphrey, who has been with Sir John for forty years and is treated more as a friend and confidant than a servant, hears with surprise his master's hushed announcement: "This wedding of my son's, in all probability—shut the door—will never be at all" (307). Nevertheless the preparations for the wedding continue. The dilemma centers on Bevil, Jr.'s ambiguous relationship with a beautiful but penniless orphan named Indiana, whom Bevil, Jr., is supporting. When Mr. Sealand, Lucinda's father, learns of Bevil's attachment to Indiana, he immediately assumes that Bevil is "already married, or worse," and he does not wish his daughter to be matched with a man already supporting a mistress. Yet Sir John Bevil himself recognizes that his son has always been the most dutiful son, scrupulously observing his father's wishes in every detail. At the same time Humphrey tells the audience that Sir John Bevil has ever been a lenient and generous father. In fact, father and son have been so attentive to each other's sensibilities as to cause each other discomfort. The father thinks that the proposed marriage, however, will be the true test of Bevil, Jr.'s fidelity, and as a result preparations continue, despite Sealand's refusal of his daughter.

What Sir John Bevil does not know is that his son is distressed by the opposing demands of obedience to his father and of love for the virtuous Indiana. Although he has supported Indiana at great expense since his discovery of her forlorn circumstances, he has never mentioned his love for her because of his strongly felt filial obligations. His father's considerable interest in a wealthy alliance suggests to Bevil, Jr., the impossibility of his father approving a marriage with Indiana. With a heavy heart but with Humphrey's assurances of eventual success, Bevil, Jr., dresses for a marriage with Lucinda.

Fortunately, Lucinda Sealand does not desire this marriage either; she is in love with Charles Myrtle, the exceedingly jealous and intemperate friend of Bevil, Jr. Assuring his friend of his honorable intentions, Bevil, Jr., sends his servant Tom to Lucinda's servant Phillis with a letter explaining his true feelings. Lucinda responds quickly with a letter acknowledging her love for Myrtle but her fear of his jealous temper. Characteristically, Myrtle perceives the letter from Lucinda to Bevil through the distorted perspective of his jealousy, and as a result he challenges his friend to a duel. Bevil, Jr., remonstrates with his friend while retaining his honor and reputation, and through reason and Lucinda's letter convinces Myrtle of his rash mistake. Steele places great importance on this argument against dueling, as he claims in the Preface: "Nor do I make any difficulty to acknowledge that the whole was writ for the sake of the scene of the fourth act, wherein Mr. Bevil evades the quarrel with his friend."

Minor complications beset Myrtle and Lucinda through the machinations of Lucinda's egotistical mother and the unwanted attentions of her coxcomb cousin, Cimberton. Mrs. Sealand desires an alliance of her daughter with Cimberton because of his great wealth. Jealous of her daughter's beauty, she would also be happy to have her far away in the country at Cimberton Hall. The successful conclusion of Myrtle's courtship comes not from his marvelous efforts at disguise, as Counselor Bramble, attorney, and then as Sir Geoffry Cimberton, patriarch, but from the solution of the major problem in the main plot, Indiana's identity. Mr. Sealand, experienced merchant and man of business as he is, decides to see Indiana for himself. In the midst of this interview she throws down a bracelet which belonged to Sealand's first wife; through this discovery Sealand identifies Indiana as his long lost daughter by his first wife, Mrs. Danvers. Pleased with Bevil, Jr.'s exemplary conduct, Sealand offers Indiana with half of his fortune to the man who loves her. Bevil, Jr., is thus rewarded with marriage to Indiana as well as his father's approval. Meanwhile, Cimberton cancels his offer to marry Lucinda because half of her fortune now belongs to Indiana; his real desire has been the acquisition of money, not love. Charles Myrtle happily comes forward to claim Lucinda, though her fortune is diminished by half. The credit for the opportune discovery of Indiana by Sealand and the happy resolution of the lovers' difficulties is given, as the play concludes, to the "secret care of Providence."

Serious Couple and Gay Couple. Readers of Restoration drama have long been familiar with the terms "gay couple" and "serious couple."[5] Certainly anyone familiar with Etherege's *The Man of Mode* and Wycherley's *The Country Wife* is aware of the ascendancy of the witty, daring, strongly independent man and woman over the more sedate, sensible, and conventional couple in those comedies. The tradition of the gay and serious couple is part of Steele's heritage as a dramatist. With his didactic and moralistic intent, one might expect that he would elevate the man and woman of sense, the serious couple, to a position of eminence, whereby they might be models for the audience. And so he does. Young Bellair of *The Man of Mode* and Harcourt of *The Country Wife* are distant cousins to Bevil, Jr., in their serious approach to love. Correspondingly, Steele demotes the gay couple, whose values he presents for comic effect, not for imitation, to the servants Tom and Phillis. He ridicules servants imitating the wit and foppery of the past age and presents the hero and heroine as chaste, serious, and reasonable models in a new and better age.

Tom and Phillis are delightfully funny characters, partly because of the absurdity of their fashionable dress and language. Their roles of gallant and mistress are as secondhand as Phillis's clothes handed down by her lady Lucinda; though Phillis may be "dressed like a woman of condition," and though Tom considers himself one of the "gentlemen who are well fed and cut a figure"—a very pretty fellow indeed—yet they are both in fact servants. Tom and Phillis are the gay couple of *The Conscious Lovers,* ridiculed for manners, language, and dress inappropriate to their condition. One may hear Richard Steele speaking through Humphrey as he replies to Tom: "I hope the fashion of being lewd and extravagant, despising of decency and order, is almost at an end, since it is arrived at persons of your quality" (311). Steele attempts to degrade this gay and witty lifestyle, offering as a positive alternative "Breeding to refine the age/To Chasten Wit, and Moralize the Stage" (304). It is not surprising, then, that Phillis's entrance appears a lighthearted parody of Millamant's entrance in Congreve's *The Way of the World,* with her "new Manteau and Petticoat" as well as "new Thoughts and new Airs with new Cloths" described by Tom with admiring appreciation. But Phillis is unworthy of Millamant: "But here she comes; in one motion she speaks and describes herself better than all the Words in the World can" (313). Phillis imitates, through her secondhand thoughts and airs and clothes, a world no longer in fashion, a manner discarded by men and women of sense.

The couples who are proposed as models of exemplary conduct, Bevil, Jr., and Indiana, Charles Myrtle and Lucinda, are, despite some slight faltering by Myrtle, men and women of sense. This description means that they are chaste, reasonable beings who understand and respect moral duty.[6] Myrtle's only fault, his rash jealousy, threatens to undermine the virtue of friendship, but at the conclusion he is cured of his weakness. Significantly, Steele chooses similar ideal qualities for both Bevil, Jr., and Indiana: chastity, reason and good sense, and benevolence and gratitude. Nowhere in *The Conscious Lovers* does Steele propose any double standard for his exemplary characters; both Bevil, Jr., and Indiana adhere to the same values. Only Mrs. Sealand and Cimberton, characters ridiculed by Steele, desire a gross subservience of wife to husband (not Mrs. Sealand for herself, naturally). While the hypocrite Cimberton uses his intellect to conceal his pride and avarice, Bevil, Jr., uses his reason as a moral guide; Steele suggested much earlier in *The Christian Hero* that reason and religion together should guide the passions to moral action, and Bevil, Jr., embodies that principle. Indiana says of him, "his Actions are the Result of Thinking, and he has Sense enough to make even Virtue fashionable" (311). Both Bevil, Jr., and Indiana recognize the importance of reason over passion in their love. Bevil, Jr., says to Indiana: "If I might be vain of anything, in my Power, Madam, 'tis that my Understanding, from all your Sex, has mark'd you out, as the most deserving Object of my Esteem," and Indiana's reply is equally definite in its exaltation of reason: "Esteem is the Result of Reason, and to deserve it from good Sense, the Height of Human Glory" (333). Bevil, Jr., describes his ideal man of sense—"what every Gentleman ought to be"—as one "who takes more delight in Reflections, than in Sensations," and one who is "more pleased with Thinking, than Eating" (336).[7] Such is Steele's serious couple, his man and woman of sense. To teach his audience the moral values embodied in these characters is indeed Steele's purpose in *The Conscious Lovers*.

The Ideal of Filial Piety. In all of his plays Richard Steele is concerned with the difficulties and obligations in the father-son relationship. The earlier plays dealt with problems arising between fathers and sons, while *The Conscious Lovers* presents an ideal relationship worthy of imitation by the audience. In *The Funeral* Lord Brumpton was the weak father who, swayed by his attachment to his new wife, sought to disinherit his faithful son. In *The Lying Lover* the situation is reversed, Young Bookwit thoughtlessly breaking his loving father's heart. In both of these plays fathers and sons are reconciled at the conclusion, so that the audience may be instructed in overcoming problems between parent and child. Steele takes a different approach in *The Tender Husband*, where Sir Harry Gubbin's overbearing and negative attitude toward his son, Humphry, reaps the expected result, a son striving for independence at all costs. The play ends with only a hint of reconciliation, neither father nor son learning or growing from experience. *The Conscious Lovers* presents a father and son who are the opposite of the Gubbins; Sir John Bevil and

Bevil, Jr., are overly considerate of each other's sensibilities so that, while they are exemplary ideals, they are also mildly amusing. Their extreme sensitivity to each other is a clever stroke by Steele, for it gives them life and interest. The servant Humphrey summarizes their personalities well: "Well, tho' this Father and Son live as well together as possible, yet their fear of giving each other Pain, is attended with constant mutual Uneasiness" (310).

Both Sir John and his son describe their manner of living with one another. Sir John's method of raising Bevil, Jr., is indeed exemplary, diametrically opposed to Sir Harry Gubbin's: "As soon as he grew towards Man, I indulg'd him in living after his own manner: I know not how, otherwise, to judge of his Inclination; for what can be concluded from a Behavior under Restraint and Fear?" (308). Such a regimen has wrought excellent results, as Humphrey clearly perceives: "You have ever acted like a good and generous Father, and he like an obedient and grateful Son." Nevertheless, though this father and son are worthy of imitation, they are not perfect. Sir John is proud of his son's dependence upon his will, despite his apparent willingness to give his son free rein. Bevil, Jr., owns his mother's great estate, yet his wealth has not encouraged independence from his father, undoubtedly to his father's liking. And yet Bevil, Sr.'s relatively minor quirk does not destroy his otherwise exemplary paternal qualities; Steele may be suggesting that such flawed goodness may be the best one can achieve in this world. Certainly Bevil, Jr., understands and respects his father's strengths and weaknesses and does not desire him better than he is. He welcomes his father with these words: "Sir, you are the most Gallant, the most Complaisant of all Parents" (317). Though a modern audience might desire it, there is not a touch of irony here. Both father and son are disposed to respect and care for each other.

The test of their mutual esteem arises through Bevil, Jr.'s love for Indiana. Sir John is anxious at Bevil, Jr.'s delay at Toulon and alarmed at his public display of concern for Indiana at the masquerade. Not suspecting his son's virtuous design, he concludes that Bevil, Jr., has married unwisely and without his consent or that he has taken a mistress. Bevil, Jr.'s marrying without his father's approval would cause a severe rupture between them, and to resolve his uncertainty Sir John insists on the marriage to Lucinda. Bevil, Jr.'s reply, though disingenuous, is true in the main: "As I am ever prepar'd to marry if you bid me, so I am ready to let it alone if you will have me" (318, 361).

The delay in arriving at a mutual understanding arises from Sir John's perplexity over his son's "Insensibility to the fairest Prospect, towards doubling our Estate" (361). Yet both Sir John's prudential interest in money and Bevil, Jr.'s love are satisfied, as Indiana receives half of Sealand's fortune. Bevil, Jr., maintains his promise not to marry without his father's consent, as Sir John joins Sealand in approving his marriage to Indiana. Sir John Bevil's prudential concern for fortune, while worldly-minded, is not satirized, for it indicates at least to some degree a practical if misguided concern for his son. Bevil, Jr.'s generous love and his father's prudence together provide an ideal for an eighteenth-century audience.[8]

The Importance of Marriage.   The mutual rights and obligations of parents and child in the choice of a marriage partner presented a topic of lasting interest to Steele's audience. Some of the most famous novels of eighteenth-century England—Richardson's *Clarissa* and Fielding's *Tom Jones,* for example—focus upon the problems resulting from an overly restrictive parent preventing a daughter's free choice. The Harlowes allow Clarissa no choice but to accept the family's avaricious will; Fielding's Squire Western, though more loving, is no more liberal toward his daughter Sophia. Steele addressed the same problem years earlier in *The Conscious Lovers,* but in the mode of exemplary drama he presented the solution to the problem. Bevil, Jr., states the principle that ensures the right of a son or daughter not to be forced into an odious and unacceptable marriage: "I never will marry without my Father's Consent: But give me leave to say too, this Declaration does not come up to a Promise, that I will take whomsoever he pleases" (321). One might have expected Steele to emphasize the importance of a mutual veto by parent and child as an essential right. In drama and essay Steele often expressed the need for sensitivity in human relationships, so the exemplary Bevil also enunciates this essential principle. Sir John Bevil's insistence on his son's marriage with Lucinda violates such a right, but he is not entirely at fault because Bevil, Jr., professes a ready willingness to do his father's will. The ideal is preserved, at the play's conclusion, as Sir John Bevil and Sealand give approval to Bevil, Jr.'s and Indiana's choice of a marriage partner. The same principle applies to Lucinda Sealand and Charles Myrtle, of course, but unfortunately they incur even greater difficulty than Bevil, Jr., and Indiana.

To some degree Lucinda's situation is not unlike Clarissa's in Samuel Richardson's novel; Lucinda's mother gives no importance whatsoever to love in marriage, retaining total control of the choice of her daughter's husband and basing her choice entirely on financial considerations. Lucinda understands that her mother is abridging her rights, as with bitterness she explains her mother's demand: "Mamma says, the first time you see your Husband should be at that Instant he is made so; when your Father, with the help of the Minister, gives you to him; then you are to see him, then you are to Observe and take Notice of him, because then you are to Obey him" (343). Further injustice has been done: Myrtle had the Sealands' approval of his courtship of Lucinda, but the opportunity of a wealthier alliance encouraged Mrs. Sealand to put an end to his pretensions. "Every Corner of the Land has presented me with a wealthy Coxcomb . . . To be barter'd for, like Beasts of the Field . . . but for encrease of Fortune," exclaims Lucinda with disgust (344). Her situation has the tragic potential of Clarissa's, except for the fact that Sealand is not a party to his wife's machinations and would not coerce his daughter into marriage. Such insurance against a disastrous marriage provides a comic potential to her difficulties with her suitors. The decrease in Lucinda's fortune by half offers Myrtle the opportunity to declare his love for her and not for her fortune: "No Abatement of Fortune shall lessen her Value to me" (379). Sealand's approval ratifies the mutual choice of Myrtle and Lucinda, again demonstrating that adherence to the principle of respecting the choice of both parent and child provides a greater assurance of a successful and happy marriage, based on love as well as prudential considerations.

Steele's Ideal Woman. The female characters in *The Conscious Lovers* have varying positive and negative qualities. Indiana and Lucinda, though differing in personality, together comprise what may be identified as Steele's ideal woman. Mrs. Sealand and Isabella, again with widely different personalities, represent what Steele considered negative in a woman's character. Phillis, because of her servant status, reveals a saucy wit and a mildly self-seeking ability to cope with the world which might be incongruous in a well-bred lady. The positive characteristics that receive most emphasis in Indiana and Lucinda are strong understanding and a thorough self-knowledge, which Steele upholds to the audience as especially worthy qualities.

Steele believed that women ought not to be relegated to ignorance and limited to household pursuits; instead women as well as men should attain intellectual growth and cultivation, and as a model for this accomplishment Indiana reveals among her other fine qualities a cultivated knowledge of literature, music, and opera. She presents, as Steele sees her, an admirable judgment in her recognition of the superiority of English drama to Italian opera: "All the Pleasure the best Opera gives us, is but mere Sensation . . . . The Musick's certainly fine; but in my Thoughts, there's none of your Composers come up to Old Shakespear and Otway" (334). Bevil, Jr., immediately ratifies her judgment by naming her a woman of sense. In her conversation with her Aunt Isabella Indiana shows herself to be the more reasonable and the less emotionally vulnerable of the two. Indiana judges Bevil, Jr.'s motives and her own emotions with surprising precision, whereas Isabella ignores her reason because of one deeply painful experience which lends a bias to her judgment.[9]

Lucinda as well shows a good understanding and a sound judgment. She evaluates her potential suitors very capably, seeing Cimberton for a pedantic coxcomb and identifying with remarkable accuracy the one fault in Myrtle, jealousy, that could ruin their marriage. Whereas Mrs. Sealand's judgment is biased by her pride in her supposed intellectual prowess, thus blinding her to the pedantic hypocrisy in her cousin Cimberton, Lucinda sees clearly both her mother's and Cimberton's weaknesses. In her dealings with Bevil, Jr., Lucinda shows spirit and intelligence, joining with him in the deception for her own as well as his happiness. Sufficient evidence of Lucinda's sound reason and judgment may be found in Mrs. Sealand's negative appraisal of her daughter: "She has, I confess, no Ideals, no Sentiments, that speak her born of a thinking Mother" (346). From an ignorant, jealous, arrogant, and avaricious person that is praise indeed!

Because of the apparently passive nature of Indiana's response to Bevil, Jr., some readers have concluded that Steele is proposing that women be totally dependent upon men. While it is true that Indiana is dependent upon Bevil, Jr., her dependence is a matter of fortune and not of character. She shows herself to be poised and assertive in her discussions with Isabella, Bevil, Jr., and Sealand. Rather than passivity Steele is proposing a cultivated mind, a sound judgment, and thorough self-knowledge as important, worthwhile qualities for women. After observing the male characters in *The Conscious Lovers,* one notices that he is proposing the same exemplary qualities for men.

Satire of Pride and Hypocrisy.   Although *The Conscious Lovers* is an exemplary comedy, it does count among its characters two who are satirized and ridiculed for their serious faults. Unfortunately, both of these characters are one-dimensional representations of pride, hypocrisy, jealousy, and avarice, no more than personifications of reprehensible character traits. Steele does not allow Cimberton and Mrs. Sealand the usual human mixture of strengths and weaknesses; these characters are as negative as Bevil, Jr., and Indiana are positive. Their potential for evil is negated, however, by the greater power of the positive characters, and thus Cimberton and Mrs. Sealand are not perceived as serious threats to the others. Steele's characterization in *The Conscious Lovers* derives from the didactic purpose of his comedy; his aim is to teach a moral lesson, not to present a realistic or even a believable human situation.

Mrs. Sealand confers lavish praise on what she terms Cimberton's learned taste and refined sense of things. As he examines

Lucinda, the woman with whom he seeks a marriage contract, Cimberton treats Mrs. Sealand to a discourse on the impediments of sex to a man of letters and speculation. Yet as he looks with gross familiarity upon his future wife, it is clear that Cimberton has lust but no love in his heart. He talks about, not to, Lucinda, and he examines her as he would a purchase, not a person. Cimberton's eyes belie his high-flown, pedantic discourse; as he condemns the honest recognition and the pleasure of sex in marriage, he at the same time leers at the outraged Lucinda: "I am considering her, on this occasion, but as one that is to be pregnant . . . . And pregnant undoubtedly she will be yearly. I fear I shan't for many years, have Discretion enough to give her one fallow Season" (347). He then has the brazenness to complain to Mrs. Sealand about the cost of feeding and clothing ten children, an expense not to his liking. Mrs. Sealand's comment is a marvelous understatement: "What an Oeconomist!" (347) These two, representative of avarice and a prurient sexuality, also represent the old wealth; significantly Sealand himself, though a merchant, is not avaricious.

Steele pokes fun at the absurd pretensions of those who scorn the valuable mercantile activities of men like Sealand. Cimberton unwittingly joins with the disguised Myrtle in scorning the merchant class, and one can almost hear Steele laughing in the background. To his supposed uncle, Cimberton says, "There's no hiding the Disgrace, Sir; he trades to all parts of the World." The false Sir Geoffry replies, "We never had one of our Family before, who descended from Persons that did anything" (366). Cimberton, of course, accepts this answer seriously. Mrs. Sealand also concurs in this disparaging and unjustified attitude, despite the remarkable achievements of her own husband. Merely by yoking his negative characters in this way, Steele suggests that a reasonably unbiased person would take a more positive attitude toward Sealand and his associates. Steele also allows Sealand to argue vigorously and effectively for the value and strength of a mercantile economy, against the doubts of Sir John Bevil.

Lest there remain any doubt about the motivation of Mrs. Sealand in disposing of her daughter, Steele has her admit her jealousy to Phillis: "I'll live no longer in anxiety for a little Hussey, that hurts my Appearance, wherever I carry her: and, for whose sake, I seem to be not at all regarded, and that in the best of my Days" (369). Mrs. Sealand's jealousy and avarice provide motivation for her interest in the Cimberton proposal, but these traits also tarnish her character sufficiently so that she and Cimberton may be appropriate spokesmen for pride of superior position as well as selfishness disguised as intellectual superiority.

Whig Propaganda. *The Conscious Lovers,* claims John Loftis, is "a vehicle by which Steele can convey the opinions he formulated in the last years of Anne, when he was one of the chief Whig propagandists."[10] Yet the tone of Steele's play is akin to the genial manner of the *Spectator,* not to the abrasive satire in his public quarrels with Swift. The pairing of Sir John Bevil and Mr. Sealand, merchant, approximates the famous members of the fictional Spectator club, Sir Roger de Coverly and Sir Andrew Freeport. In both works the Whig merchants have the best of the argument, demonstrating that with their clear-thinking, hard-working, progressive, and empirical approach to life they are the foundations of England's economy. These successful, intelligent mercantile leaders are essential to England's future, at least according to Steele's firmly held convictions.

Steele felt that a dialogue between Sir John Bevil and Mr. Sealand, representing their relative social positions, was sufficiently important to warrant inclusion in his play.[11] Sir John opens the final negotiations for the marriage of his son to Sealand's daughter with an assertion that genealogy and descent are of some consideration; he thus reveals his pride in his family heritage, unwarranted because he has in no way earned his status. Sealand counters with a not-very-good joke—about the lineage of dogs his father kept, which he shows to be as meaningful—or meaningless—as Sir John's. The country Tory thinks he will now defeat Sealand's argument with certainty, as he says: "I never knew any one, but he that wanted that Advantage, turn it into ridicule." Sealand replies with wit and grace, effectively diminishing the value of a social register: "And I never knew any one, who had many better Advantages, put that into his Account"

(358). The Whig creed that Steele is preaching calls for individual accomplishment, that self-same industry so well promoted by Benjamin Franklin, reader of the *Spectator* papers. Sir John Bevil, though genteel, pleasant company and an ornament to society, is a relic of a past age; one may assume that Bevil, Jr., will use his talents more industriously than does his father.

Steele turns the argument then to moral issues, where Sir John loses his footing quickly: "Sir, I can't help saying, that what might injure a Citizen's Credit, may be no Stain to a Gentleman's Honour." Once again Sealand overwhelms Sir John's muddled thinking: "Sir John, the Honour of a Gentleman is liable to be tainted, by as small a matter as the Credit of a Trader" (359). [12] Sealand equates honor and credit, thus eliminating any superiority of the gentleman and suggesting that both are signs of honesty and reliability. Sealand also criticizes the double standard of sexual morality, which Sir John assumes as a gentleman's prerogative; not only must gentleman and citizen be judged by the same moral standards, urges Sealand, but men ought to adhere to the same sexual standards as women. This is the argument Steele had been proposing since *The Christian Hero;* though Sir John attempts a sneer, he is unable to dispute Sealand's argument.

Having gained the arguments on genealogy and on morality, Sealand now makes his concluding, decisive statement, which Sir John does not try to question: "We Merchants are a Species of Gentry, that have grown into the World this last Century, and are as honourable, and almost as useful, as you landed Folks, that have always thought your selves so much above us" (359). (One notes the incisive yet delicate irony in the words "almost as useful.") This is the conclusion toward which Steele has been aiming all along. Lest any question remain about Sealand's cultural interests, Steele has his merchant quote John Dryden, the greatest writer of the last age, as proof of his acquaintance with literature and, presumably, the theater. The discussion between Sir John and Sealand leaves no doubt about the intellect and integrity of the merchant Sealand; if superiority exists, it belongs to Sealand, based as it is on individual ability and accomplishment.

The Duel Scene, or the Benevolent Victor. John Harrington Smith said it bluntly but correctly: "Steele personified benevolence in Bevil, Jr. in *The Conscious Lovers.*"[13] And yet Bevil, Jr., goes beyond benevolence, "wishing well," in order to demonstrate beneficence, "doing well." This distinction is important, for charitable promises masquerading as benevolence are the very stuff of hypocrisy, of which Bevil, Jr., is not guilty. Instead he follows in virtuous action the dictates of a benevolent mind and heart. Steele, like Fielding, had no patience with those who promised but performed not; Steele looked for charity in deeds rather than words. Bevil, Jr., demonstrates this practice in a variety of situations.

The most obvious acts of beneficence take place before the play's commencement, as Bevil, Jr., rescues Indiana by paying for her liberty and returning her to England. Bevil, Jr., relates them to Humphrey, and in so doing diminishes their value by his modest self-evaluation. Nevertheless, these acts of virtue, performed "not without some Difficulty," deserve recognition; there is no suggestion that the audience should doubt the sincerity of Bevil, Jr.'s motives. Certainly Bevil, Jr.'s treatment of Indiana upon her return to England is beneficent as well as benevolent; he not only feels indulgent and protective toward her, but he also pays for her lodging and entertainment and demonstrates active concern for her welfare.

Bevil, Jr., feels as much obedience and filial respect for his father as love and concern for Indiana. Indeed, Bevil, Jr.'s dilemma—the central focus of the plot—is founded in these opposing obligations. Nevertheless, through the dialogue between Humphrey and Sir John Bevil, the audience learns that Bevil, Jr., has never in word or deed appeared independent of his father. This would be the less remarkable except that the father undoubtedly wishes his son dependent and that the son is in fact an independently wealthy landowner with title to his deceased mother's great estate. For a financially independent young man to repress his inclinations out of respect for his father is noteworthy, especially as it is without selfish intent. Bevil, Jr., shows an aggressive concern for his father at the masquerade, as he provokes an open struggle with a clownish young man teasing Sir John Bevil. Bevil, Jr.'s filial piety is an active, not a passive, quality.

Bevil, Jr., presents the ideal of beneficent friendship in his treatment of Charles Myrtle and Lucinda Sealand. His plain-dealing non-courtship of Lucinda is noteworthy. While it is true that breaking a marriage agreement with Lucinda will benefit his own future marriage plans, Bevil, Jr., knows that Lucinda's happiness depends on Myrtle and that his professed lack of interest will allow Lucinda and Myrtle to proceed in their courtship. Lucinda values young Bevil's plain dealing without taking offense at his rejection of her: "Never was Woman so well pleased with a Letter, as my young Lady was with his" (341). Unfortunately, Charles Myrtle does not perceive Bevil, Jr.'s plain dealing as clearly, biased as he is by an apparently uncontrollable jealousy. A most difficult test of Bevil, Jr.'s beneficence arises with his friend Myrtle's unquenchable doubts about Bevil, Jr.'s motives and plans for Lucinda. While the scene (act 2, sc. 1) provides the groundwork for Myrtle's later challenge to a duel, at the same time it reveals the essential nature of Bevil, Jr.'s friendship. Although Sir John Bevil's demands force his son to appear ready to marry Lucinda, young Bevil has generously shared with his friend Myrtle his secret resolve never to marry her.[14] Yet Myrtle needs reassurance again and again that Bevil, Jr., will indeed keep his promise; when, however, Bevil, Jr., requests his friend's help to escape the match, Myrtle angrily demands why Lucinda is unworthy. Bevil, Jr., had he been so inclined, could have demanded redress of injury to his honor through a duel with his friend, but instead he mollifies his friend's anguish with kind good humor while ignoring temporarily his own impending difficulties. Even the easily upset Myrtle calls him a "reasonable and good-natur'd Friend." Minutes later, however, Myrtle is once again upon the rack, doubting his friend's fidelity. Myrtle's recurring distrust of his friend, caused by overwhelming jealousy, provides the motivation for his challenge of Bevil to a duel; Steele states in his Preface that Bevil's evasion of this duel on honorable terms is the most important part of the play.

Steele's further claim that "the whole was writ for the sake of the Scene of the Fourth Act" (299) is sometimes underestimated. The duel scene between Bevil, Jr., and Myrtle not only represents Steele's proclamation by example of the absurdity of dueling, but it also serves as a capstone to Bevil, Jr.'s beneficence in action. Steele hopes that the evasion of the quarrel may have a positive "Effect upon the Goths and Vandals that frequent the Theatres," emphasizing his belief that an audience will imitate what it sees upon the stage. Equally important, then, is the exemplary nature of Bevil, Jr.'s benevolence and beneficence, which serve as ideals for the audience. Reason is the guide to Bevil, Jr.'s benevolence, and by the coolness of his reason he is able to convince Myrtle of his rash and unfounded jealousy. In addition, through the admonition against jealousy in Lucinda's letter, it is likely that Myrtle may be cured of his infirmity by this extreme embarrassment. Myrtle learns the essential lesson of this scene, derived from his friend's good deeds throughout the play which Steele wishes the audience to observe: "There is nothing manly, but what is conducted by Reason, and agreeable to the Practice of Virtue and Justice" (357).

Lawyers, Grimgribber, and Disguise.   In both *The Funeral* and *The Conscious Lovers* Steele satirizes, with obvious pleasure, the language and antics of lawyers. In his last play he merges his satiric treatment of lawyers with his surprisingly funny use of sight comedy and disguise. These scenes balance the sententious dialogue elsewhere in the play. Steele is remarkably adept in both the serious and the satiric modes.

Bevil, Jr., suggests the use of disguise to Myrtle as a way of protracting Cimberton's financial arrangements before marriage to Lucinda. Myrtle assumes the disguise of Counselor Bramble, and Tom, Bevil, Jr.'s servant, becomes Serjeant Target, both lawyers involved in the settlement of vast estates. The audience, of course, takes obvious delight in their deceiving Cimberton and Mrs. Sealand, and Steele provides a deftly appropriate touch as Cimberton relishes his own plan of deception immediately after being completely deceived.[15] The language of this scene suggests that Cimberton deserved, perhaps even invited, such treatment because of his condescending attitude toward others and his willing acceptance of deception as the way of his world.

Deception is the way of the world for lawyers, suggests Steele, and thus the meaningless gibberish spoken by Myrtle and Tom is accepted by Mrs. Sealand and Cimberton as the veritable language of the law. Myrtle and Tom invent an argument about the "Messuage of Grimgribber" which allows them to speak to each other rather than to Cimberton and Mrs. Sealand. Having asked one simple question and received Grimgribber in reply, Mrs. Sealand remains humbly silent before the apparently learned discussion of these two frauds.[16] She supposes that this is the baffling discourse of all lawyers, designed to intimidate rather than to communicate.

Steele's satire on lawyers did not stop at this point, but descended into buffoonery. Target is given a speech defect, both to further impede communication and to give him an absurd air: "Yes, Madam, we have agreed that it must be by Indent-dent-dent-dent-." Steele realizes that mockery of Target's stuttering, low comedy at best, shows questionable taste, but he defends his choice by claiming that an attorney who is "extremely Passionate, and impatient of Contradiction" deserves ridicule; Target does not have the physical or emotional qualifications for an attorney, and his impertinence exaggerates his defects.[17] Steele's satire on lawyers is severe. The disguised Myrtle and Tom have spoken gibberish, acted with hauteur and arrogant pride, and shown themselves incompetent, and yet both Mrs. Sealand and Cimberton assume that they are truly lawyers.

The Recognition Scene. The recognition of Sealand and Indiana as father and daughter was a most touching scene for an eighteenth-century audience, and yet critics then and now have argued about its lack of verisimilitude. By the improbability of the plot's resolution the play moves away from "truth to life," suggests Ernest Bernbaum. "That perfectly virtuous people come to a happy issue out of all their afflictions is, alas, a theory not so plausibly illustrated in a world resembling the real one as in a realm of beneficent coincidence."[18] Two problems arise here. Steele's exemplary comedy is not designed to resemble the real world but to teach a fallen world ideals worthy of aspiration. Steele believed wholeheartedly in the teaching function of the drama and thus developed exemplary drama. Moreover, he believed in Divine Providence and in a God who rewarded virtue here and hereafter. The discovery of father and daughter may thus be seen as a reward of virtue after trial and difficulty. The recognition scene has little meaning if it is only the result of "beneficent coincidence." The reuniting of father and daughter attains its proper significance only when perceived as a result of beneficent Providence, a reward of virtue and part of a design, not simply an accident. Steele announces this context for the recognition scene, as Sealand exclaims: "O! Sir John! how vain, how weak is Humane Prudence? What Care, what Foresight, what Imagination could contrive such blest Events, to make our Children happy, as Providence in one short Hour has laid before us?" (378) Sir John Bevil echoes the same trust in Providence as the play concludes: "Whate'er the generous Mind it self denies, The secret Care of Providence supplies" (379). The deity of this play—and by implication of the real world—is involved in human events, but in mysterious and sometimes unknown ways, so that a rigidly dispensed poetical justice is neither observed in the real world nor in the world of the play. Seen in this context, the recognition scene serves a meaningful purpose as evidence of the workings of Providence; its primary use is not for sentimental effect. It serves appropriately as the completion of Steele's lesson on ideal virtue and the conclusion of his exemplary—and providential—comedy.

Chapter Four

Morality Tempered by Wit: The Achievement of the *Tatler*

The *Tatler*

On April 12, 1709, Steele began a paper called the *Tatler,* which quickly became the talk of the town. For his reputed author, Steele borrowed the character Isaac Bickerstaff invented by Jonathan Swift to satirize the quack astrologer Partridge, but he developed Bickerstaff much more fully for a different purpose. Whereas Swift made one man the butt of a joke, Steele aimed to improve the society of London and its environs by means of a gentle, laughing satire. "The general purpose of this paper," according to Bickerstaff in the Dedication to Arthur Maynwaring, "is to expose the false arts of life, to pull off the disguises of cunning, vanity, and affectation, and recommend a general simplicity, in our dress, our discourse, and our behavior."[1] Such a design would be more successful under the name of a fictitious character, as Steele well knew; the town would not take kindly the strictures of Richard Steele, known for his jovial, active life about town.[2] By using a persona Steele not only had greater freedom for his commentary but also could invite friends to participate in writing *Tatler* papers. His most famous collaborator was his good friend from childhood, Joseph Addison. Addison participated in the Bickerstaff characterization very capably, adjusting comfortably to Steele's perception of his persona. But despite Addison's large contribution, the *Tatler* is Richard Steele's creation and achievement.

Isaac Bickerstaff was by no means a transparent mask for Steele; indeed, Bickerstaff assumes a life and personality of his own, becoming a central focus of the *Tatler*. Bickerstaff reveals the garrulity of an old man talking about past experiences, fashions, family and friends, and women. Though a bachelor, he takes great pleasure in discussing various difficulties in marriage. Admitting that he is sixty-three years old, Bickerstaff enjoys his position of senior statesman on the topics of love, marriage, dueling, honor, and life in general. The commentary on politics, though minimal, appears more as the remarks of Steele than as the lucubrations, as he liked to term them, of Isaac Bickerstaff. Steele must have felt a strong urge to venture into political propaganda, but fortunately he erred in this direction rarely, and then relatively subtly for Steele.[3] The persona of Bickerstaff remained intact until the very end, when in *Tatler* 271 Steele signed his name and announced that he had "nothing further to say to the world, under the character of Isaac Bickerstaff."

Steele provided Bickerstaff not only with a fully developed and slightly eccentric personality but also with a circle of friends foreshadowing the club of the *Spectator* and an incredibly large and facetiously named family.[4] Bickerstaff's club is an unusual collection of oddities, brought together by age and eccentricity. Spending every evening with these drowsy old men, Bickerstaff establishes his own eccentricity as well as his age. Among his friends are Sir Jeffrey Notch, a gentleman of ancient family, Major Matchlock, a long retired soldier, and Dick Reptile, a good-natured, indolent old man; these friends entertain each other with the same stories and jokes every night. The reader may laugh at these oddities while at the same time accepting Bickerstaff as a believable old man, not by any means perfect, but still perceptive and considerate of his friends. As a result, the relationship between reader and Bickerstaff is non-threatening, with Bickerstaff generous to his friends' foibles and restrained in his own eccentricities. And yet Bickerstaff is far from incompetent; his words have a practical and useful wisdom. Steele's Bickerstaff was soon receiving voluminous mail, some of which was answered in publication.[5]

Bickerstaff's family provides an additional humanizing influence for Steele's persona. The most important member is Jenny Distaff, Isaac's half-sister and junior by forty years, who writes several papers. The remainder of the family form a topic for conversation and a source of correspondence. From Humphrey Wagstaff came the poems "Description of the Morning" (no. 9) and "Description of a City Shower" (no. 238); Bickerstaff's ingenious kinsman of course is Swift. Isaac enjoys telling stories about his ancestors, such as Sir Isaac the Knight of the Round Table, Sir Walter who married the milkmaid, and Mrs. Margery who had a thousand pounds to her portion, which her family was desirous of keeping among themselves, and therefore used all possible means to turn her thoughts from marriage (no. 197).[6] They are as varied a group as most relatives, some worth claiming, some not. By describing his relatives in such amusing detail Bickerstaff wins the friendship of his readers, inducing them to expect more yarns about his family and to compare his to their own. Steele hit upon an excellent method of establishing a warm rapport between author and reader.

This character adopted from Swift became radically changed under the guiding pen of Richard Steele. Initially Steele used the Bickerstaff name because it was known by the town, but although Partridge is mentioned from time to time Steele moved his persona away from astrologer to physician for manners and morals.[7] As early as *Tatler* 7 Steele began to indulge Bickerstaff's playful eccentricities: Bickerstaff complains that he has "not a month's wit more" and therefore makes out his will, distributing not only property but also his qualifications, learning, and wit. Adroitly shifting his topic to marriage, Bickerstaff claims that a marriage he recently attended was so melancholy that he "took a resolution to forbear all married persons . . . for four and twenty hours at least." With this witty, unpredictable, and happily eccentric character, it is no surprise that readers were curious to see what would come next.

Plan, Purpose, and Tone. As the *Tatler* commenced, Steele's plan provided five departments as areas of focus for different types of news or essays. Coffeehouses of some reputation provided locations for Steele's departments: "All accounts of gallantry, pleasure, and entertainment, shall be under the article of White's Chocolate-house; poetry, under that of Will's Coffeehouse; learning, under the title of Grecian; foreign and domestic news, you will have from St. James's Coffee-house; and what else I shall on any other subject offer, shall be dated from my own apartment" (no. 1, pp. 12–13). At this time Steele was editor of the *London Gazette,* the government news publication, and he could rely on news dispatches to provide material for the *Tatler* as well. Once readers began to respond to Bickerstaff in some numbers, however, Steele found less need for a news section and moved more and more often to single essays dated from his own apartment or from his address in Shire Lane. The plan developed beyond his original conception as the Bickerstaff persona took on greater importance and as readers responded to Bickerstaff with letters and requests for advice.

Through Bickerstaff 's genial and understanding lessons, Steele proposed both to reform and to entertain. The light touch of his satire and the unpretentiousness of his ethical discussion made the lessons of the *Tatler* not only palatable but pleasurable. Announcing his intention, he says, "I must go on cheerfully in my work of reformation: that being my great design, I am studious . . . that we may not give vice and folly supplies" (no. 30). His intent is clearly didactic. Though his attitudes should appeal to a mature audience, much of his advice is directed to a younger audience involved with courtship, love, and marriage. Giving moral guidance to his readers involved Bickersatff in criticism of faulty deportment, and he often threatens his readership with publication of their secret follies: "As we have professed, that all the actions of men are our subject, the most solemn are not to be omitted, if there happen to creep into their behavior anything improper for such occasions" (no. 54). Ridicule of faults, however, could easily become tiresome, and as a result Bickerstaff discusses methods of satire and indulges in various approaches to improving behavior.

Ridicule, of course, had been the traditional mode of criticism for vanity and hypocrisy; it was agreed, however, that no one should be criticized for deformities of character that are not within one's power to correct: "By the rules of justice, no man ought to be ridiculed for any imperfection, who does not set up for eminent sufficiency in that way wherein he is defective" (no. 63). A different mode of improving mankind—one which Steele used in *The Conscious Lovers*—is the presentation of idealized characters worthy of imitation; this method is recommended to Bickerstaff by a correspondent who says, "I cannot but applaud your designed attempt of raising merit from obscurity, celebrating virtue in distress, and attacking vice in another method, by setting innocence in a proper light" (nos. 71, 74).[8] A reply to this suggestion reaffirms the primacy of ridicule and satire in a work of reformation, charging "that whilst we laugh at, or detest the uncertain subject of the satire, we often find something in the error a parallel to ourselves" and through this awareness and consequent shame achieve a correct behavior (no. 76). Bickerstaff practices both of these modes in fact, often presenting through anecdote or story virtuous characters but even more often depicting faulty aspects of characters otherwise similar to his readers. His primary method of satire and correction may be summarized thus: "We shall therefore take it for a very moral action to find a good appellation for offenders, and to turn them into ridicule under feigned names" (no. 61).

The tone of Bickerstaff's satire is distinctly Horatian, designed to produce laughter and improvement rather than bitterness and despair.[9] The lightness in his attitude is notable early in the *Tatler:* "New persons, as well as new things, are to come under my consideration. . . . But it is my design, to avoid saying anything, of any person, which ought justly to displease" (no. 4). Even his lightness might become tiresome, however; fortunately Steele varied his tone from issue to issue and often within issues. This variation of subject matter, tone, and attitude—Bickerstaff is even stern at times—gives the *Tatler* qualities that encourage continuing interest.

Men and Morals. One of Steele's aims throughout the *Tatler* was the definition and analysis of exemplary male qualities. These, not ancestry or wealth, are the true qualifications of a gentleman,

Steele firmly believed, and praise of worthy gentlemanly characteristics became a commonplace among readers of the *Tatler*. Bickerstaff constructs a model of the ideal gentleman, adding little touches here and there, based on the qualities of good nature, self-respect, honor, and benevolence. Often he will mention these qualities only at sufficient length to leave an impression on a receptive mind. For example, in a discussion of satire, he reminds his readers that good-natured men have ever "a frankness of mind, and benevolence to all men" (no. 242). At other times his emphasis falls on moral choice: "To contradict our desires, and to conquer the impulses of our ambition, if they do not fall in with what we in our inward sentiments approve, is so much our interest, and so absolutely necessary to our real happiness, that to contemn all the wealth and power in the world, where they stand in competition with a man's honour, is rather good sense than greatness of mind" (no. 251). The theoretical bases for any proposed moral action are the reformed passions, aided by religion and reason, as described in *The Christian Hero*. Steele refers to the reformed passions as inward sentiments, which, because of their redirection by religion and reason, are now able to guide men to correct moral choices. True good nature is directed by these impulses to beneficence without any thought of reward or applause (no. 138). The only reward—more gratifying than public praise—is the conscious enjoyment of a good action.

Bickerstaff becomes more radical than this, however, in his commands to moral action. He ridicules the accepted practice of dueling, and he replaces the double standard of sexual morality for men and women (widely agreed upon by men, at least) with a moral imperative of chastity for both sexes.[10] "It is certain," says Bickerstaff, "that chastity is a nobler quality, and as much to be valued in men as in women" (no. 58). One may imagine the derision this statement met with, and yet Bickerstaff continued to promulgate modesty as a "certain indication of a great and noble spirit" (no. 86). This is, of course, the major theme of *The Conscious Lovers,* Steele's last and most successful comedy, but it recurs in various forms throughout the *Tatler*. Steele and Bickerstaff recommend religion as the proper guide to modesty and chastity: "Thus humble, and thus great, is the man who is moved by piety, and exalted by devotion" (no. 211). Enjoinders of the positive commands of conscience suggest the same chastity, piety, and conscious beneficence for both men and women.

Bickerstaff places true virtue and honor in the quality of a man's actions, not the quality of his ancestors, and considers rank and status in life an unreliable indicator of true quality. For example, in describing the values of a country life, he accords respect to a country gentleman because of his virtuous actions, not his possessions: "There is no character more deservedly esteemed than that of a country gentleman, who understands the station in which heaven and nature have placed him. He is father to his tenants, and patron to his neighbors, and is more superior to those of lower fortune by his benevolence than his possessions" (no. 169). The principle upon which Steele bases his respect for a country gentleman is the equality of all men until their lives are distinguished by virtue or vice. "Fortune shall no longer appropriate distinctions," says Bickerstaff, "but Nature direct us in the disposition both of respect and countenance" (no. 180). This belief is consistent with Whig political theory, and Steele advances this skeptical attitude toward hierarchy and distinction with subtle effectiveness.[11]

Insofar as the family is the microcosm of the state, Steele's commentary on parenting offers a useful illustration of the mutual respect that develops between parent and child, or ruler and ruled, when the one wielding power allows freedom of thought and action. With some relish Bickerstaff tells a story of a father who, concerned by his son's extravagant and distressing behavior, decided to give his son £4000 and, "by giving him opportunities of tasting what it is to be at ease. . . ," to encourage his son to accept responsibility (no. 60). The resulting improvement of the relationship, one can be sure, warmed Steele's benevolent heart.[12] Later Bickerstaff describes the congenial relationship between a father and his two sons. This father allows his sons their freedom, and they in turn treat him with loving respect: "Their father is the most intimate friend they have, and they always consult him rather than any other" (no. 189). Unfortunately, many parent-child relationships do not approximate this ideal, and consequently Bickerstaff sternly berates parents who try to control every moment of their children's lives. He supports his position with a story about his cousin Samuel Bickerstaff and his two children. Says Isaac of the son and daughter: "Their life is one continued constraint" (no. 189). It is apparent that these children have no freedom and therefore no respect for their tyrant. This lesson, which applies to King James II in 1688 as well as to Samuel Bickerstaff, is directed "to those parents who seem to make it a rule, that their children's turn to enjoy the world is not to commence till they themselves have left it" (no. 189).

As he did with his cousin Samuel, Isaac Bickerstaff corrects a variety of faults by depicting and sometimes ridiculing the offending action or mannerism. Both manners and morals receive his critical comments, with a range from ogling to murder. Much of the time manners and morals overlap in Bickerstaff 's critiques; in general, however, his primary aim is to teach a practical morality based on good works, and thus his emphasis falls on analyzing and often solving realistic, even mundane, problems and questions. Though his method often is ridicule of a faulty action or mannerism, the alternative positive mode of behavior is clear both to Bickerstaff and his readers. For example, when he criticizes the troublesome behavior of Very Pretty Fellows and Smart Fellows, who are "familiar among the ladies, and dissolute among the rakes" (no. 24), he places this pretension to wit and good breeding in contrast with true wit and good humor. All pretenders to qualities they do not command, all persons who are affected and thus dishonest in their relationships with others are fair targets for Bickerstaff 's satire. The rake, the coxcomb, the pedant, and the sharper all come within his purview.

Bickerstaff 's didacticism is not always specific and directive, however; he asks his readers to think for themselves, to assume responsibility for self-directd moral behavior, and not to imitate unthinkingly the latest fashion, whether in clothing or in behavior. Those who refuse to think for themselves are enrolled in the lists of the "dead": "Whoever resides in the world without having any business in it, and passes away an age without ever thinking on the errand for which he was sent hither, is to me a dead man to all intents and purposes. . . . The living are only those that are some way or other laudably employed in the improvement of their own minds, or for the advantage of others" (no. 96). This ridicule of those better fed than read hearkens back to Swift's denunciation of Partridge as "no man alive," which Steele echoes in *Tatler* 96. Steele expands the criticism to a threat—good-natured, of course—against unthinking followers of fashion.

Another favorite group for criticism includes those whom Bickerstaff terms "dogs" and "sharpers," men without honor or conscience who prey upon the naive and innocent part of mankind: "I shall in my future accounts of our modern heroes and wits, vulgarly called 'sharpers,' imitate the method of that delightful moralist [Aesop]; and think, I cannot represent those worthies more naturally than under the shadow of a pack of dogs . . . made up of finders, lurchers, and setters" (no. 59). Bickerstaff returns often to this theme, receiving a letter from Bath complaining about the dogs there (no. 65), another letter about dogs who specialize in biting young heirs whose states are entailed (no. 66), notice of dogs with dice at Bath (no. 68), and even descriptions of the meaner dogs in the kennels (no. 70). His satirical description of the various kinds of sharpers and gamesters— all dogs—is amusing and instructive. In a paper designed to explain Bickerstaff 's dictum that "every worthless man is a dead man," Joseph Addison emphasizes the serious aspect of Bickerstaffian satire, dismissing as a "false opinion that what I write is designed rather to amuse and entertain than convince and instruct" (no. 96).

The instruction which forms the backbone of the *Tatler*—the binding, one might say—was designed to improve mankind by helping men realize their potential for good. "The great end of education," says Bickerstaff, is "to raise ourselves above the vulgar" (no. 69). He speaks not about ambition, but about quality of life; he claims that "vulgar" refers not to the condition of life a man is in, but to a man's behavior, thoughts, and sentiments. Although it is a "common error of considering man as a perfect

creature" (no. 92), nevertheless mankind may strive toward improvement with reasonable hope; upon this hope is based the
moral teaching of the *Tatler*. Steele put into practice in the writing
of the *Tatler* the advice which he gave his readers, namely, "to
turn their thoughts to practical schemes for the good of society,
and not pass away their time in fruitless searches" (no. 261).

Women, Morals, Love, Marriage. In the *Tatler's* discussion
of love, marriage, and women, Steele uses two personae instead
of one in order to add a female perspective. Jenny Distaff, Isaac's
half-sister, assumes a dual role; she is both a writer of *Tatler*
papers about love and marriage and a character experiencing joy
and difficulty within marriage. Jenny is a convincing writer and
an appealing character, but whether Steele expresses accurately
a female perspective on the issues of love and marriage is doubtful.
He rationally favored education of women, mutual respect between a man and woman in marriage, and a single standard of
sexual morality for men and women; at the same time, however,
he was emotionally tied to a more conservative attitude toward
women, shown by his numerous quotations from Milton on marriage as well as his belief that a woman should be the helpmate
of man. [13] For Steele, the ideal woman accepted her traditional
role in marriage while still pursuing educational and intellectual
achievement.

Among Jenny's achievements is her ability to write papers at
least as interesting as her brother's; her writing style is irre-
proachable. At the same time she does not meddle with the Latin
epigraphs at the head of each paper, for that is clearly Isaac's
prerogative. In her pursuit of marriage Jenny represents Steele's
ideal woman; although she falls into pride and affectation temporarily, she has the good sense to accept her brother's temperate
advice and to correct her behavior. All the while, of course, her
errors are considered frailties typical of women and her good sense
is founded in her acceptance of male perceptions of ideal female
behavior in marriage.

Jenny's only radical statement arises over the widely accepted
double standard of sexual morality. Contemplation of this injustice arouses her indignation; speaking of a hard-core practitioner

of the double standard and his unfortunate wife, she says, "He intends she shall be a cuckold; but expects, that he himself must live in perfect security from that terror. He dwells a great while on instructions for her discreet behavior, in case of his falsehood" (no. 10). Later she returns to this topic, encouraging "the happiness of well-governed desires, orderly satisfactions, and honourable methods of life" and deploring the derision of the "most amiable term in human life," the name of wife (no. 33). This theme, common to all of Steele's writings, is most advantageously presented in *The Conscious Lovers* and *The Funeral,* but Steele did not find the argument sufficiently compelling to follow it in his younger days.

Jenny and her husband Tranquillus do practice what she preaches; moreover, Jenny gracefully accepts Isaac's advice about her deportment in marriage. The bachelor Bickerstaff claims that most of the marriages he has seen have been unhappy and that "the great cause of evil has proceeded from slight occasions" (no. 79). Precept is less effective than experience. Tranquillus and Jenny have their first argument about two weeks after their marriage, while still visiting her brother. Bickerstaff performs the office of mediator by expostulating with Jenny about her superior bearing toward her husband. Indeed, the argument itself is not discussed; instead, Bickerstaff urges Jenny "to avoid snap-dragon" with her husband and by her complaisant behavior to retrieve his happiness (no. 85). By this method Jenny and Tranquillus return to their real inclinations, namely, to live together peacefully.

During the following spring Jenny once again falls into error, and once again her brother is the mediator who explains her mistake. The overly fond and generous Tranquillus allows his wife her own equipage, an extravagant expense for one of his fortune. He "bade me want for nothing that was necessary," says Jenny, and to her that meant a coach, horses, and pride over her neighbors (no. 143). Bickerstaff's method in this case is to strengthen the husband's control over his wife by admonishing him firmly with a letter against frivolous expense. In all, however, Jenny and Tranquillus have a happy marriage, which Bickerstaff appreciates with a benevolent heart. As Jenny expresses her hap-

piness with Tranquillus, her brother prepares a friendly admonition: "An inviolable fidelity, good humour, and complacency
of temper outlive all the charms of a fine face, and make the
decays of it invisible" (no. 104).

Jenny certainly approximates Steele's concept of an ideal
woman, but through Bickerstaff's other discussions of women
Steele suggests additional characteristics worthy of consideration
by his female readers. Bickerstaff's friend speaks of his wife as
an "inestimable jewel," a woman signalized by her good humor,
gentleness, and sprightly conversation (no. 95). Aspasia too receives Bickerstaff's highest praise; she is a "female philosopher"
who seeks retirement and contemplation, a most exact economist
who is virtuous yet not proud (no. 42). Caelia offers another
perspective of the ideal woman, the image of beauty and grace
imbued with religious piety and devotion. Through these descriptions Bickerstaff creates a model woman designed for the
edification of his readers. In Bickerstaff's teaching the moral and
the practical merge.

Bickerstaff shows considerable respect for a thinking woman,
one who by her education and good sense merits the roles of
"friend, companion, and counsellor" as well as wife (no. 159).
Using letters from Pliny and Cicero, he invokes the authority of
the ancients to encourage mutual respect and good will between
husbands and wives. He expresses great appreciation for tranquillity in domestic life: "Everyone admires the orator and the
consul; but for my part, I esteem the husband and the father"
(no. 159). At the same time, he places the responsibility for a
tranquil home life upon the wife: "I think most of the misfortunes
in families arise from the trifling way women have in spending
their time, and gratifying only their eyes and ears, instead of
their reason and understanding" (no. 109). Almost one year later
Bickerstaff proposed a ladies library as a resource for education
of women on moral and religious topics. With or without this
aid, however, the burden of regulating a household and ensuring
domestic tranquillity while demonstrating unfailing piety and
good sense remained woman's lot.

Bickerstaff spent considerable ink attacking female pride, vanity, and affectation; he despised coquettes and he disliked wives who flaunted their power over their husbands. As he relates the story of a weak-tempered husband ruled by his wife—"She therefore took upon her to govern him, by falling into fits whenever she was repulsed in a request, or contradicted in a discourse"—Bickerstaff reveals contempt for both husband and wife (no. 23). "What is the proper method of handling such a conflict?" one may ask Bickerstaff. A husband must exert his authority, the censor would say, as this woman's second husband does, wonderfully curing her of her fainting spells. Bickerstaff applies his ridicule to coquettes as well: "As a rake among men is the man who lives in the constant abuse of his reason, so a coquette among women is one who lives in continual misapplication of her beauty" (no. 27). The coquette Cynthia is "an ungrateful woman, who triumphs in her falsehood, and can make no man happy, because her own satisfaction consists chiefly in being capable of giving distress" (no. 107). This trait of conscious hard-heartedness earns Bickerstaff's criticism whether it occurs in a man or a woman. It is apparent that he finds pride—in Scripture the chief of the seven deadly sins—offensive in both men and women, though perhaps more so in women. His attack on the platonic ladies suggests his considerable opposition to proudly independent women (no. 32). Although he approved further education and instruction of women and mutual esteem between husbands and wives, he did not wish women's subordinate position in relation to men changed.

One of Bickerstaff's more famous reflections concerns the love inspired by Aspasia in all who observe her: "To behold her is an immediate check to loose behaviour; and to love her is a liberal education: for, it being the nature of all love to create an imitation of the beloved person in the lover, a regard for Aspasia naturally produces decency of manners, and good conduct of life in her admirers" (no. 49). As Bickerstaff describes it, love has a strong influence on moral behavior, in its ideal setting preparing a man and woman for marriage and moral responsibility. Elsewhere he separates love and lust into irreconcilable opposites, love being altruistic and lust entirely selfish. The highest exemplum of love Bickerstaff depicts appears in the story of Paetus and Arria, in which Arria chooses death because of her love for her husband. The average English couple were not likely to face such a trial, but the consistent advice about the importance of love, Bickerstaff hoped, might have some positive effect upon their consciousness. While advising a correspondent about choosing a husband, he recommends a man with qualities inspiring love and esteem despite his lesser fortune (no. 200). Choosing love before money was not ordinary in early eighteenth-century England, and Bickerstaff 's advice may have inspired many a thoughtful discussion among those approaching marriage.

If Bickerstaff 's correspondent acceded to his advice, then she would experience in marriage the type of love recommended in the *Tatler*. A marriage based on mutual esteem is likely to inspire trust (no. 136) as well as a sense of partnership. Despite Bickerstaff 's acceptance of women's subordinate social position, he suggests that as human beings one is not superior to the other: "The soul of a man and that of a woman are made very unlike. . . . Our minds have different, not superior qualities to theirs" (no. 172). His argument is designed to promote mutual respect and benevolence, and ultimately love. [14]

The initial attraction of a man and woman may arise from reason or emotion, but the long lasting tie of a happily married couple derives from the passion of love guided and improved by reason and religion. The pathetic story of the death of his friend's wife, told by Bickerstaff with strong feeling, illustrates the completeness of his friend's love and binding emotional attachment to his wife (nos. 95, 114). The experience of this powerful force— call it love, passion, or attachment—is together with religious devotion the highest and best of human life for Bickerstaff. Such a belief in the potential beauty and delight of marriage permeates the *Tatler*'s discussion of marriage and love.

Dueling, Drunkenness, and Freethinking. After his duel against Captain Kelly, Steele waged a lifelong struggle against the custom of dueling in defense of courage and honor. Through a series of papers in the *Tatler* Isaac Bickerstaff ridicules what he considers an absurd practice. In *Tatler* 25 he translates a formal challenge to a duel into "plain English": "Because you want both breeding and humanity, I desire you would come with a pistol in your hand, on horseback, and endeavour to shoot me through the head; to teach you more manners. If you fail of doing me this pleasure, I shall say, you are a rascal. . . ; if you will not injure me more, I shall never forgive what you have done already." Through a compliment received from a correspondent about a month later, Bickerstaff suggests that his ridicule is effecting a reduction in duels; he takes credit for "rooting out from amongst us that unchristianlike and bloody custom of duelling" (no. 38). He also approaches his subject with lighter, subtler satire, as he describes his own dueling practice. It seems that the sixty-three-year-old Bickerstaff had been threatened by sharpers he had criticized in print, and as a result decided to study and practice self-defense. His occasional references to his continuing difficulties with his dueling exercise make the subject silly, encouraging laughter and derision from the reader. To try to laugh dueling out of fashion was probably at least as effective as objecting to it in a formal and serious way, as Steele did in *The Conscious Lovers*.

With a similar approach Bickerstaff satirizes drunkenness, eliciting his readers' laughter at his own dilemma. The unfortunate old man had sat for four hours, drinking claret with a merry group, engaging in buffoonery and dull humor. Nothing in the conversation was interesting or memorable; in fact, Bickerstaff says, "I remember nothing" (no. 45). With the satire at his own expense, Bickerstaff can hardly be criticized for moralistic discourse, and yet his lesson is effective in educating his readers. Later in the *Tatler* Bickerstaff assumes a serious tone in his attack on drinking: "As he who drinks but a little is not master of himself, so he who drinks much is a slave to himself. . . . I ever esteemed a drunkard of all vicious persons the most vicious" (no. 241). Bickerstaff adds drunkards to his list of the dead, claiming that the age of thirty-three is "the grand climacteric of a young drunkard" (no. 241). Nonetheless, he allows and even encourages the enjoyment of wine, although he still inculcates prudence in its use: "It is shocking in nature for the young to see those whom they should have an awe for in circumstances of contempt" (no. 252).

Bickerstaff's attack on freethinkers shows a consistent reverence for Christianity, though not for minute discussions of dogma or for zealous intolerance. In addition to prescribing due reverence in church and the avoidance of the habit of swearing, he argues that a belief in a deity and Providence is essential for a right-thinking Englishman: "The persons who now set up for free-thinkers, are such as endeavour by a little trash of words and sophistry, to weaken and destroy those very principles, for the vindication of which, freedom of thought at first became laudable and heroic. These apostates, from reason and good sense, can look at the glorious frame of Nature, without paying an adoration to Him that raised it" (no. 135). These emotionally charged words, amplified by a series of clauses defending the soul, Providence, omniscience, and the afterlife, reveal Steele's position on the Christian religion. For Steele and many of his contemporaries, this was indeed an age of religion.

Louis XIV, Marlborough, and the War.   Steele proved himself steadfast in both his loyalties and his hatreds. Among those winning his admiration, perhaps the chief was John Churchill, Duke of Marlborough, the leader of the allied attack against France in the War of the Spanish Succession. Among the objects of Steele's lifelong antipathy were Louis XIV of France and the Catholic church, representatives of political and religious absolutism. In the early days of the *Tatler* Steele's lavish praise for Marlborough was generally acceptable. The political divisions in 1709 had not yet taken irreversible positions on Marlborough, and Steele's praise could thus be taken simply as patriotic fervor (nos. 5, 6, 46, 64, 65). The humorous attacks on Louis XIV of France may be seen in the same light, as the reaffirming of the traditional English disdain for the French absolute monarchy. Toward the end of 1709, however, political change came at a rapid pace, and praise of Marlborough and mockery of the French king could no longer be published in the *Tatler* without encouraging political reaction and dispute. To keep the *Tatler* apolitical, the praise of Marlborough and the supposed correspondence with the French king eventually ended.

The fabricated correspondence with the French king bears examination, for Steele uses his persona Bickerstaff effectively in establishing a saucy tone as he discusses serious matters. The first letter, which Bickerstaff claims was stolen from France, relates the poverty and suffering of the French people under the domination of a senile, helpless old king (no. 19). The second is supposedly a letter from Isaac Bickerstaff, who signs himself "Thy generous Enemy," to the King of France; with emotional fervor and rhetorical flair he admonishes the Sun King: "Awake, O monarch, from thy lethargy! Disdain the abuses thou hast received: pull down the statue which calls thee immortal: be truly great: tear thy purple, and put on sackcloth" (no. 23). The position of Bickerstaff as competent astrologer, wise old man, and reasonable, moderate Englishman offers greater authority to this mocking foolery about Louis XIV. Realizing that his satire had to be facetious and light in order to be accepted, Bickerstaff invents a poem from his kinsman "Bread, the Staff of Life" to the king of France about the poverty and hunger of his French subjects. As Bread tells his cousin, I "have not been seen there [France] these many months" (no. 24). As the laughter began to die down in early June, 1709, readers of the *Tatler* (who were probably watching intently for the next installment) were treated to a fabricated letter from Louis XIV himself to Isaac Bickerstaff, much of it irrelevant but concluding with an invitation to France. Bickerstaff laughs at the invitation, suggesting that he would probably be locked in the Bastille (no. 26). Shortly thereafter Bickerstaff publishes a supposed letter from the people of France to their king, with a seditious admonition: "Absolute power is only a vertigo in the brain of princes, which for a time may quicken their motion, and double in their diseased sight the instances of power above them; but must end in their fall and destruction" (no. 29). With this Bickerstaff's satire takes on the appearance of serious and somewhat dull political propaganda. By June, 1710, almost one year later, his tone changes completely, now that Louis XIV, like Marlborough, held symbolic importance for party factions.

Sounding very much like Richard Steele, a loyal Whig, Isaac Bickerstaff writes again to Louis XIV about the French king's preference for the Tories: "Your writers are very large in recounting anything which relates to the figure and power of one party," says Bickerstaff, "but are dumb when they should represent the actions of the other" (no. 190). Mockery of the French king is forgotten in the attempt to discredit the other party, the Tories. Swift, as one might expect, saw this mud-slinging for what it was, and replied in *Examiner* 2: "I protest I know no man in England but him [Bickerstaff] that holds a correspondence with his Christian Majesty [Louis XIV]."[15] And so the witty, facetious fooling about Louis XIV in the early papers ends in party strife, unfortunately and unnecessarily tarnishing the *Tatler's* relatively apolitical reputation. Steele, in short, loses control of his persona as well as his tone.

Milton and Shakespeare. With surprising regularity Steele incorporated a practical criticism of the works of Milton and Shakespeare, offering in the *Tatler* an acquaintance with Shakespeare's plays and Milton's *Paradise Lost* for the novice as well as astute and appreciative commentary for the well read.[16] Except for the mention of "Comus" in *Tatler* 98, Steele has Bickerstaff focus on *Paradise Lost,* and his major interest, as Richmond Bond points out, is neither Satan nor Adam, but Eve, who becomes for Bickerstaff a representative of all women. Often using quotations from *Paradise Lost* as illustrations of a theme, Bickerstaff studies the idea of married love presented by Milton through Eve. With praise for "so chaste and elegant a manner," Bickerstaff presents "Hail wedded love" as a paean to marriage and its potential joy. Earlier he had asserted Milton to be promulgator of disinterested love, or passion in repose. Milton's words, "Adam with looks of cordial love / Hung over her enamoured," elicits this reaction, which emphasizes the altruistic and generous nature of love while deemphasizing sexual passion: "'This is that sort of passion which truly deserves the name of "love," and has something more generous than friendship itself; for it has a constant care of the object beloved, abstracted from its own interests in the possession of it'" (no. 40). Later he examines Adam and Eve as a married couple with ordinary disagreements and discussions, as in the argument from the ninth book which Bickerstaff humorously renders in the "domestic style" (no. 217). Bickerstaff returns to this argument again in *Tatler* 263, expanding the quotation and emphasizing Eve's dependence upon Adam. Obviously, this theme was congenial to Bickerstaff, for it appears in different form in *Tatler* 149, where he relates a scene from the eighth book of *Paradise Lost* in which Eve absents herself from "studious thoughts abstruse." Bickerstaff refers to this "as a lecture to those of my own sex, who have a mind to make their conversation agreeable as well as instructive, to the fair partners who are fallen into their care." Milton makes it clear that Eve, though fully capable of understanding intellectual discourse, chooses to be dependent upon Adam; similarly Bickerstaff recommends that wives be instructed by their husbands, as Eve is by Adam.

Bickerstaff appears as Milton's defender against Dryden in *Tatler* 114, where Milton's variety of language and turns of expression are praised: "The variety of images in this passage is infinitely pleasing, and the recapitulation of each particular image, with a little varying of the expression, makes one of the finest turns of words that I have ever seen; which I rather mention, because Mr. Dryden has said in his preface to Juvenal, that he could meet with no turn of words in Milton." Bond points out that *Paradise Lost* had not yet gained its great fame, so that Bickerstaff was indeed leading the way in its appreciation. [17]

The references to Shakespeare reflect the considerable popularity of Shakespearean dramas as well as the recognition of his superior craftsmanship. Bickerstaff refers to a large number of plays, including *Richard III* (no. 90), *Hamlet* (nos. 106, 111), *Othello* (nos. 167, 188), *The Taming of the Shrew* (no. 231), *Macbeth* (no. 167, 251), and *Julius Caesar* (no. 53). His respect for Shakespeare's talents may be discovered from Bickerstaff 's comment in a discussion of *Julius Caeser:* "Shakespeare is your pattern" (no. 53).

Drama Criticism. It is no surprise that Steele's interest in the theater permeates the *Tatler,* nor is it curious that he attempts to interest his readers in the drama and the stage. Steele's persona, Bickerstaff, claims to be old friends with actors, theater managers, and writers, so that in his lucubrations he offers a sense of intimacy with the theater. One may sense Steele's voice behind Bickerstaff 's in the apology for the discussions of the theater: "It may possibly be imagined by severe men, that I am too frequent in the mention of the theatrical representations; but who is not excessive in the discourse of what he extremely likes?" (no. 182). With this warm and congenial tone Bickerstaff presents his perceptions about theatrical representations, theories of acting, imitation and didacticism, and poetic justice.

Bickerstaff approves not only serious theater but the gaiety and pleasure of an audience enjoying the spectacle of lights, scenery, dress, and action. He even admits how his eyes wander from the stage to the audience: "I confess it is one of my greatest delights to sit unobserved and unknown in the gallery, and entertain myself either with what is personated on the stage, or observe what appearances present themselves in the audience" (no. 182). In general, however, Bickerstaff manages to attend to what is transpiring on stage, and he rejects buffoonery, mime, ladder-dancing, and the like as replacements for the rational pleasure of a stage presentation in English. He believes that drama ought to appeal to the mind as well as to the sight, so that both tragedy and comedy may provide moral instruction. One should leave, says Bickerstaff, with "a livelier sense of virtue and merit than he had when he entered the theater" (no. 99). The great actors Hart and Mohun, having instilled this conviction in Bickerstaff, "never failed to send me home full of such ideas as affected my behaviour, and made me insensibly more courteous and humane to my friends and acquaintance" (no. 99). Experiencing a theatrical production appeals to both the rational and emotional in humankind, but for Bickerstaff "ideas" cause him to modify his behavior and to achieve moral improvement. Moral didacticism is an essential aspect of the drama as it is discussed throughout the *Tatler.*

For Bickerstaff no one could be a better representative of the highest acting abilities and best qualities of the theater than Thomas Betterton. Nearing seventy-four years of age, Betterton was still able to act Hamlet in 1709, embodying "the force of action in perfection," exuding the "power of proper manner, gesture and voice" (no. 71). The artistic expression so masterfully presented by Betterton tended to "dwell strongly upon the minds of the audience," and, according to Bickerstaff, "would certainly affect their behavior." Less than a year later Betterton was dead, and *Tatler* 167 is devoted to Betterton and his wife. Bickerstaff describes Betterton as "a man whom I had always very much admired, and from whose action I had received strong impressions of what is great and noble in human nature." The emotionally powerful descriptions of Betterton's accomplishments on the stage lead irresistibly to praise of the theater as an institution: "There is no human invention so aptly calculated for the forming a free-born people as that of a theatre."

Bickerstaff offers free lessons on acting, and his directions are pointed and specific. At one time he quotes Hamlet's directions to the players as an ideal worthy the attention of all actors (no. 35). Later he praises an actor's ability to adjust his voice and countenance and yet appear natural and without distortion (no. 51). In addition he praises a specific actor, who "by the grace and propriety of his action and gesture, does honour to a human figure" (no. 115).[18] Both his instructions and his praise are designed to improve an actor's ability to communicate through the medium of his art, thus fulfilling more effectively drama's chief aim, the instruction of the audience. This indeed is the purpose of an "accomplished player." "The apt use of a theatre," recommends Bickerstaff, presents "the most agreeable and easy method of making a polite and moral gentry" (no. 8). Bickerstaff is committed to a theory of imitation by the audience of the moral action depicted on the stage, a theory which justifies the existence of theater on both utilitarian and moral grounds. By assuming an affective purpose, the institution of the theater exists not for itself but for its audience, the receiver of drama's moral suasion. Bickerstaff argues in a later *Tatler* that "The opposition of right and wrong on the stage would have its force in the assistance of our judgments on other occasions" (no. 182). His model for the theater is drama as moral education.

As a result of this belief Bickerstaff rejects poetic justice, punishing the evil and rewarding the good, because the intelligent spectator knows such a disposition of rewards does not resemble human life.[19] Poetic justice may be logical and appealing, but it is neither true nor realistic. Experiencing unmerited suffering vicariously through the drama affects the mind and heart of the observer positively, claims Bickerstaff, because it teaches sympathy "for the great misfortunes and calamities incident to human life." Bond recommends Bickerstaff's discussion of poetic justice as "one of the most interesting critical passages in the *Tatler.*"

The *Tatler* has a moral purpose similar to the theater's, and one may speculate on the relative ease Steele felt in moving from writing comedies to periodicals. Within the *Tatler* there is a description of a greenhouse which may in various ways symbolize the workings of Steele's periodicals and comedies upon the human spirit. But that is another subject.

The Restful World of the Greenhouse. Although the country and its diversions offer only a minor divertissement in the *Tatler,* Isaac Bickerstaff is warmly responsive to the beauties of nature, especially in milder and more domesticated aspects. He delights himself as well as his readers with a pleasant ramble in the imagination: "To stand by a stream, naturally lulls the mind into composure and reverence; to walk in shades, diversifies that pleasure; and a bright sunshine makes a man consider all nature in gladness, and himself the happiest being in it, as he is the most conscious of her gifts and enjoyments" (no. 169). One who enjoys these pleasures of nature with his heart is characterized by "benevolence, civility, social and human virtues."[20] Part of Bickerstaff's goal in the *Tatler* is the promulgation of mild, civilized virtues, such as benevolence and good nature. His almost lyrical description of the taming and domestication of nature—the preservation and emphasis of its mild, benevolent, soothing aspects—in a magnificent greenhouse (no. 179) appears emblematic of the moral didacticism throughout the *Tatler,* which converges on one purpose, the improvement, cultivation, and preservation of the mild and beneficent human passions.

This greenhouse replaces for correspondent T. S. the savage, egoistic, diversions of riotous eating and drinking, wenching, gaming, racing, and hunting, as well as pride in equipage and apparel. Instead, T. S. enjoys throughout the year the mild sights and sounds of nature protected from wintry blasts. With his family and friends he participates through his senses in the improvement of his mind and passions: "I never enter this delicious retirement, but my spirits are revived, and a sweet complacency diffuses itself over my whole mind. And how can it be otherwise, with a conscience void of offence, where the music of falling waters, the symphony of birds, the gentle humming of bees, the breath of flowers, the fine imagery of painting and sculpture: in a word, the beauties and the charms of nature and of art court all my faculties, refresh the fibres of the brain and smooth every avenue of thought" (no. 179). So it is with the *Tatler,* which offers a soothing retirement, with the possibility of improvement and refreshment, helpful indeed in dealing with daily cares. "This place likewise keeps the whole family in good humour, in a season wherein gloominess of temper prevails universally in this island." Humankind is a part of physical nature, as an individual person is a part of society or social nature. The effect of the *Tatler* upon readers may have been similar, one may imagine, to the effect of the greenhouse upon T. S. and friends: "My greens and flowers are as sensible as I am of this benefit: They flourish and look cheerful as in the spring."[21] The entertainment of his neighbors is "the chief pleasure of all," and so too for Richard Steele in the *Tatler.*

The wintry blast of political discontent, an unfortunate attack on Robert Harley, the *Examiner*'s continued sniping, and Steele's own weariness of his persona all contributed to the ending of the *Tatler* with number 271 on January 2, 1711. "I am now come to the end of my ambition in this matter," wrote Steele over his own name. The abrupt ending of the *Tatler* did not mean that Steele and his friend Addison were weary of periodical writing or of commentary on society. Indeed, the opposite is true, for in a very few months these two friends would begin the *Spectator*, perhaps the outstanding periodical of its kind in English literary history.

Chapter Five

The Achievement of Richard Steele as Mr. Spectator

The *Spectator*, begun on Thursday, March 1, 1711, was a joint achievement by Richard Steele and Joseph Addison, with contributions from many other sources.[1] Nevertheless, Steele is often identified as the major writer with Addison as his mainstay helper.[2] On Saturday, December 6, 1712, Steele signed his name to *Spectator* 555, the final number of the original publication, thanked Addison for his assistance, and credited their other friends who wrote papers. Even Mr. Spectator's physical appearance, especially his very short face, was identified with Steele's. Despite this popular perception, Addison's contribution of original material was greater than Steele's, as Donald Bond has demonstrated.[3]

Steele's use of letters is a major difference in form from Addison's use of original essays. Steele's design is generally based on dialogue with a correspondent, whether fabricated or real, which allows commentary on supposedly actual events or experiences. This model operated satisfactorily for Steele because his primary purpose was ethical teaching, a practical moral didacticism intended to appeal to a variety of readers and affect their daily lives. The *Spectator*'s quick attraction of a considerable following attests to the success of his plan.[4]

Although discussion of ethical issues dominates the pages of the *Spectator*, some commentators on the *Spectator* give Mr. Spectator's Club the most important place. The Club certainly is interesting, but it is not central either to the form or the didactic mode of the majority of the essays; in fact, the only character integrated psychologically in the essays is Mr. Spectator himself, a highly successful creation. The other members of the Club— Sir Roger de Coverly, Sir Andrew Freeport, Will Honeycomb, Captain Sentry, the templar, and the clergyman—provide a framework for Mr. Spectator's discussions with his readers.[5] Essays focusing on Sir Roger and Sir Andrew, often subtly political in tone and purpose, usually favor Sir Andrew and the interests of the Whig party. In general, the *Spectator* provided more discussion of topics generated by characters and readers and depended less on the development of family or club members than the *Tatler*.

In *Spectator* 336 a correspondent praises the spectatorial authority wielded by Mr. Spectator in his essays, and it is this sense of authority in moral concerns that is a prime characteristic of the whole of the *Spectator,* recognized by writer and reader alike. Whether Captain Sentry discusses an event of some perplexity, or Mr. Spectator quotes a sermon by John Tillotson, Archbishop of Canterbury, the goal is usually similar: to inculcate in readers a sound ethical judgment.[6] In consequence, the discussion in this chapter will focus on some issues and areas of interest that Steele found important as topics for spectatorial authority.[7] The *Spectator* "'set up the Immoral Man as the Object of Derision.' On this fundamental issue," says Donald Bond, "Addison and Steele were completely united."[8] They felt no need to apologize for ethical didacticism.

The Character of Mr. Spectator

One of the major causes of the *Spectator*'s success, a reader may reasonably speculate, is the character of Mr. Spectator. Here is a persona who also participates actively in many of the events and descriptions in the *Spectator*'s pages, a character who is a bundle of contradictions, a self-deprecating but contented member of the Ugly Club. Mr. Spectator enjoys his role as silent observer, even relishing the reactions to his oddity, while at the same time professing great pleasure in his Club's congeniality and conversation. Here, indeed, is a man for all moods! He is a likeable recluse, a sociable humorist, a talking oxymoron. His self-deprecation about the shortness of his face, his frank confession of his Ugly Club membership, and the appropriateness of his mistress, Hecatissa, are sources of laughter and admiration, for he appears like kin to an average reader. His audience came quickly to appreciate Mr. Spectator's sociable attitude and detached perspective.

Mr. Spectator's discussion of clubs, such as the Two-Penny Club, the Ugly Club, and Club of Lovers, offers a delightfully absurd description of human oddities, and he apparently relishes the opportunity for humor. Writing to the President and Fellows of the Ugly Club, Mr. Spectator salutes them with, "May it please your Deformities" as he thanks them for his admission to the Club. A letter from Hecatissa to Mr. Spectator intimates that there are "some that have Honesty and Fortitude enough to dare to be ugly" and requests admission to the Ugly Club.[9] The joke goes on, earning the reader's appreciation and perhaps acceptance of his or her own less than harmonious appearance.

In contrast, Mr. Spectator is also able to discuss the serious difficulties of life as well as the pathos of human pain and suffering. He advocates a sober acceptance of life: "We should not form our Minds to expect Transport on every Occasion but know how to make it Enjoyment to be out of Pain" (no. 143). Later he admonishes his readers to expect pain and suffering in life: "It is certainly the proper Education we should give our selves, to be prepared for the ill Events and Accidents we are to meet with in a Life sentenced to be a Scene of Sorrow (no. 312).[10] It is this multifaceted, sometimes contradictory, mask/character who attracts readers to the spectatorial authority of the essays, as he leads readers to the other members of the Club, to the ruminations of his creators, and to spectatorial wisdom.

Sir Roger de Coverly and Sir Andrew Freeport

When one thinks of the *Spectator,* one inevitably thinks of Sir Roger de Coverly and Sir Andrew Freeport, both members of Mr. Spectator's Club and yet polar opposites in social and political loyalties. The identification of the *Spectator* papers with Sir Roger and Sir Andrew is curious, since the Club participates in only a small minority of the 555 papers. Because of their appeal, however, these two representatives of the Tory and Whig perspectives of English life in 1710 have become a tradition, mentioned in the same breath with the *Spectator* papers themselves, and certainly before the short-faced Mr. Spectator. More significantly, these two knights offer a visual concreteness for many readers, a particularity which is difficult to forget, especially in Sir Roger's case. Sir Roger de Coverly, a lovable but for the most part incompetent eccentric, engages the reader's tender regard even as the Tory political positions that he espouses are slowly and subtly eroded in the same reader's opinon. While the expression of political convictions in the *Spectator* papers may have been remarkably mild by contemporary standards, the Whig political attitudes held by Addison and Steele are by no means hidden. In discussions between Sir Roger and Sir Andrew on political and social topics, Sir Andrew's Whig view prevails. There are, in addition, a number of papers by Steele that amplify a variety of topics arising from Sir Andrew Freeport's mercantilist philosophy.

First, though, a look at Sir Roger. Steele gives the reader a succinct yet effective description of the country gentleman who is antiquated more in his ideas than in his age (he is, after all, only fifty-six). Sir Roger, the spokesman for the Tory view of politics and society, is part of the last age, literally in the cut of his clothing and metaphorically in the cut of his Tory ideas. He is firmly identified with the Restoration age of Lord Rochester, Sir George Etherege, and Charles II, a pre-Glorious Revolution time of whose morals and politics Steele did not approve. He is also a part of a tradition that demands dueling for honor, a tradition which, as we have seen, Steele did his utmost to overcome. To say that "he is rather beloved than esteemed" is indeed to damn with faint praise, for it suggests that Sir Roger is beloved in spite of his incompetence. Careless about his appearance as well as his finances, Sir Roger attributes a life spent in no very great accomplishments to being "Crossed in Love, by a perverse beautiful Widow of the next Country" (no. 2). How could one want a man so easily overwhelmed by adversity, even in love, to have any responsibility for ruling England? Of course, that is unthinkable. Sir Roger is relegated to explaining a passage in the Game Act, and, hints Richard Steele, so it should be with all Tory partisans. The identification of Sir Roger with Tory ideas and ideals offers effective political propaganda and satire.

Steele's further descriptions of Sir Roger at home talking about his ancestors and his unsuccessful suit for the perverse widow are humanizing: the reader understands and sympathizes with Sir Roger's feelings. But rarely does the reader identify with him. He is too much the oddity, unlike Sir Andrew, who unites the commonly respected traits of English merchants. The descriptions of Will Wimble, a friend who is a useless hanger-on, and Moll White, a poor old woman thought to be a witch, only add to the picturesque nature of Sir Roger's life in the country, a chapter out of the past. The future belongs to Sir Andrew and his brethren. Sir Roger's description of his ancestors' pictures effectively reduces the importance of ancient lineage, upon which many old families based their social pride. Even Sir Roger chuckles at his family. More subtly damaging is Sir Roger's description of his Perverse Widow, who is apparently interested in a variety of intellectual activities and who, he claims, "understands every thing." He has such respect for her intellect that he exclaims, "I'd give ten Pounds to hear her argue with my Friend Sir Andrew Freeport about Trade" (no. 118). Is it not likely that the intellect of this wealthy widow helps her to see Sir Roger as a relic of the past, of historical interest only? For a woman of dynamic intellectual interests, Sir Roger could not possibly be considered an appropriate mate (nos. 107, 109, 113, 118).

Sir Roger's counterpart, Sir Andrew Freeport, is less easily visualized, for he is Steele's idealized portrait of many common characteristics. Sir Andrew's memorableness lies in his ideas and attitudes, not in his personality or idiosyncrasies. In numerous essays Steele amplifies the pro-merchant ideas of Sir Andrew, either through Mr. Spectator or through letters from correspondents. One quickly notices Steele's obvious pleasure in promoting a mercantile philosophy congenial to practical Whig politics. Nevertheless, Sir Andrew's is a serious philosophical position for

Steele, and it is nowhere better expressed than in *Spectator* 174. In this paper Sir Roger and Sir Andrew debate the relative value of men in trade, with Sir Roger asking "what can there great and noble be expected from him whose Attention is for ever fixed upon ballancing his Books, and watching over his Expences"? Much of Sir Roger's brief argument is phrased in questions with supposedly obvious answers; he assumes that nothing great or noble may be expected from a mere accountant. In contrast, Sir Andrew's lengthier argument is composed of emphatic, smoothly mellifluous declarative sentences which overwhelm Sir Roger's flimsy assumptions from the start. By the conclusion of this debate Sir Andrew is in such firm control that he ends with this resoundingly unanswerable declaration: "He deserves the Estate a great deal better who has got it by his Industry, than he who has lost it by his Negligence." The argument is saved from divisiveness by Mr. Spectator's opening paragraph, in which he proclaims the mutual dependence of the landed and trading interest: "The Trader is fed by the Product of the land, and the landed Man cannot be cloathed but by the Skill of the Trader." It is perhaps symbolic of larger movements in English life that toward the end of the *Spectator,* after Sir Roger's death, Sir Andrew retires from trade in order to purchase an estate in the country. Even Sir Roger's own estate passes to Captain Sentry, a soldier with an understanding of contemporary events. The changes recorded in the *Spectator* were but a microcosm of similar changes taking place through much of the early eighteenth century in England.

To some degree Steele acted as a proselytizer for attitudes favorable to mercantile activity; through the authority of Mr. Spectator he was a force in changing, very gradually, the lives of many Englishmen. The importance of contractual promises, obvious to a trader, Steele expands to all areas of life, the trivial as well as the consequential. Mr. Spectator confesses to laxity in keeping social promises, yet he recognizes the single importance of keeping one's word: "The first Steps in the Breach of a Man's Integrity are much more important than Men are aware of " (no. 448). The reputation of a merchant is founded on his integrity, which is dependent on his ability to keep promises. A merchant's reputation, however, is also liable to the calumny of casual unkindness, dislike, or jealousy; by this reminder Mr. Spectator emphasizes the importance of speaking the truth for all people in all sectors of society.

Steele also combines a quiet praise of mercantile virtues with a subtle criticism of the common faults of the wealthy, landed gentry. The beneficence of a good trader is contrasted to the self-gratification of a typical country squire, with the obvious recommendation that readers imitate the prosperous yet humane trader. The appeal made to Mr. Spectator's readers is similar to the appeal of characters worthy of imitation in *The Conscious Lovers.* In the *Spectator,* however, Steele is able to divide recommended traits into such small components that his didactic purpose does not overwhelm the larger purpose and pleasure of each essay, whereas in the more limited compass of *The Conscious Lovers* he of necessity presented his entire moral lesson in a single unified plot. A teacher of moral ideals, Steele nonetheless remained true to his purpose in whichever medium he was working.[11]

Will Honeycomb and Restoration Values

Steele's opposition to the modes and mores of Restoration comedy is well known; the design of his comedies, especially *The Conscious Lovers,* leaves no place for the libertinism of such plays as *The Man of Mode.* The method of his attack on Restoration values, adjusted to the medium of the *Spectator,* is akin to his satire on Tory political and social values. For his Tory satire Steele created Sir Roger de Coverly; for his satire on Restoration values he created Will Honeycomb, an antiquated rake who, like Sir Roger, lives in the past, in a world that lost its vitality after the accession of William and Mary in 1688.

His description of Will Honeycomb shows Steele to be contemptuous of Restoration fine gentlemen in general and especially of one who has outlived his age and still acts the part of youth: "Time has made but very little Impression, either by Wrinkles on his Forehead, or Traces in his Brain" (no. 2). Once having established the mark of his ridicule, however, Steele relaxes his attack, concluding with doubtful praise: "Where Women are not concerned, he is an honest worthy Man." In later essays Steele uses Will Honeycomb's approval of men of wit and pleasure about town as a certain indication to the reader of his own disapproval. In *Spectator* 151 he deplores the vices exemplified by Dorimant in *The Man of Mode;* at the same time, "Will thinks the Town grown very dull, in that we do not hear so much as we used to do of these Coxcombs." Steele finds it difficult to be witty on this subject, and thus Mr. Spectator grows serious as he contemplates Will's concept of wit and pleasure: Will's "Man of Wit and Pleasure was either a Drunkard too old for Wenching, or a young lewd Fellow with some Liveliness, who would converse with you, receive kind Offices of you, and at the same time debauch your Sister or lye with your Wife." As he attempted in his final play, Steele strives to develop the concept of a fine gentleman in a modest Bevil, Jr., rather than in a rakish Dorimant.

Later in the *Spectator* Steele finds himself able to shed the seriousness, which was to be endemic to *The Conscious Lovers,* and accomplishes his objective with ridicule. Will Honeycomb, so goes the story related by Mr. Spectator, was greeted familiarly by a wench of the town one rainy night when he was with Sir Roger. The joke goes against Sir Roger, who struck up a conversation with her in all innocence, but the ridicule falls only on Will, "who disguises his present Decay, by visiting the Wenches of the Town only by Way of Humour" (no. 410). Yet, even as Restoration immorality is criticized and Will himself ridiculed, Mr. Spectator tolerantly accepts Will as a harmless ladies' man whose conversation adds some spice and liveliness to their otherwise serious discourse.

The satire on Restoration attitudes toward sexual morality permeates the *Spectator* beyond the characterization of Will Honeycomb. A letter from Simon Honeycomb in *Spectator* 154 explicates the career of a repentant rake who lived in the mode of men of pleasure about town and discovered its emptiness and sham. Simon explains that he was in the twenty-seventh year of his age and forty-seventh of his constitution, with his health and estate wasting very fast, when he met a virtuous woman who reclaimed him. After their marriage Simon looks back on the life he has led and feels only revulsion; his purpose in writing the letter is, of course, to help others avoid his errors. Choosing to reaffirm the moral of this paper, Steele includes on the following Friday another letter to Mr. Spectator, this one from an antiquated Restoration rake who has not repented his former life. He accuses Mr. Spectator of undermining the fundamental maxims of life prevailing in the "joyous Reign of Charles the Second," and he asserts with aged arrogance that "it is monstrous to set up for a Man of Wit, and yet deny that Honour in a Woman is anything else but Peevishness" (no. 158). To confirm his opposition to the *Spectator,* he asserts that Mr. Spectator's discourses are the "very Bane of Mirth and good Humour." The correspondent's tone and attitude provide their own satire of the letter's contents, so that Mr. Spectator need make no comment. [12] In other papers Steele satirizes wits of the last age, the double standard of sexual morality, aged rakes who risk the highest friendship for their own selfish pleasure, and the man who symbolized pleasure-seeking throughout the Restoration, King Charles II himself. [13]

Charles II is, of course, intimately identified with Restoration comedy, his mistress Nell Gwyn acting on the stage, and his friends like Rochester understood as models for the rakes of his day. In *Spectator* 65 Steele took the direct approach in attacking the character of the rake-hero who appeared to be a hero for the audience. His specific allegations are leveled against Dorimant in *The Man of Mode:* "Our Hero, in this Piece, is a direct Knave in his Designs, and a Clown in his Language. . . . This whole celebrated Piece is a perfect Contradiction to good Manners, good Sense, and common Honesty." For Steele, *The Man of Mode* represents all that is morally corrupt in the drama of the last age; whereas his attack on the Restoration drama is direct and unmitigated and his satire on Will Honeycomb is relatively gentle and tolerant, his purpose throughout is the same—to reform the morals of the present age by eliminating any vestiges of the sexual attitudes and mores of past years. He is even willing to criticize a scene in his first play, *The Funeral,* written a little more than ten years earlier, which offends by its similarity to the sexual suggestiveness of Restoration comedy. Steele agrees, in *Spectator* 51, that "such an Image as this ought, by no means, to be presented to a Chaste and Regular Audience," and he deleted the offending materials from later editions of *The Funeral*.[14] Steele's positive goal in his reforming movement is to portray a character which he would call "The Fine Gentleman." In *The Conscious Lovers* he is Bevil, Jr.; in the *Spectator* he appears not as a unified character but as a series of characteristics recommended to the reader by spectatorial authority.

The Love Game

Using the guise of spectatorial aloofness and objectivity that Mr. Spectator wears so comfortably, Steele demonstrates a continued concern with the problems of courtship and marriage, on which he could write from experience. His benevolent interest made it natural for him to protest against courtship based on monetary interest exclusively, against marriage arranged by parents without sensitivity, and against marriage partners who abuse their mates through selfishness and lack of love. Steele's objective was to keep courtship and marriage from becoming a trap, or worse, a prison which destroyed happiness and ruined lives. Instead, he envisioned marriage as a union based on mutual consent and affection which in its ideal form would promote the happiness and personal growth of both husband and wife. Because he believed a wife should be submissive to her husband, he did not call for equality in marriage; nevertheless, he perceived that a true union could not be based on a master/slave relationship, and as a result he emphasized love and trust as essential components for a successful marriage. His *Spectator* papers on marriage reveal his special interest—one might call it his major concern—with this area of critical social importance.

The *Spectator*'s most famous example of courtship and love as a trap is the Inkle and Yarico story, in which Thomas Inkle, an English merchant, was saved from death after a shipwreck in America by the love of the Indian maid Yarico. She protected him for several months, until an English ship approached the coast, at which time Inkle asked Yarico to accompany him to

England and to live in splendor. Once safely on board, Inkle began to reflect upon his situation, especially with regard to money; upon these considerations, "the prudent and frugal young Man sold Yarico to a Barbadian Merchant" (no. 11). In a distant way, the Inkle and Yarico story resembles the trapping of the female by the male with specious promises in order to gain favorable financial settlements, a sad tradition reenacted many times in ordinary English courtship. In a later *Spectator,* Steele uses a letter from Dorinda to describe her own similar situation, a suitor careful of his fortune refusing to marry because of the smallness of hers. Dorinda laments, "I always thought he lived in a near Manner to lay up what he thought was wanting in my Fortune to make up what he might expect in another" (no. 402). For her suitor, financial considerations overrule his passionate love; while he would like her as a mistress, he does not wish her as his wife. But Steele sees even greater perfidy possible in the courtship ritual; in *Spectator* 423 Mr. Spectator himself writes a letter to Gloriana, warning her of a plot by two friends, Damon and Strephon, who design to charm her into Strephon's arms. The plot is calculated and cold-hearted, for both men perceive the courtship as a hunt. Indeed, as he warns Gloriana, these two men do "cast Lots for the Conquest." By such stories Steele attempts to alarm young women and instruct young men against a system of courtship that may bring them permanent unhappiness.

The lure of money appears to Steele the major cause of many unhappy marriages; a marriage contracted for mercenary reasons has little chance of success. This is a rather drastic change from the attitude prevalent during the Restoration, which placed prudential considerations at least on a par with feelings of love. By no means does Steele disregard financial settlements, but he does point out in various essays that mutual respect and good will should be more compelling reasons for a marriage than lust for financial gain. Mr. Spectator's story of Favilla paints a graphic picture of misery in marriage, all in the service of wealth: "Favilla . . . is marry'd to a sullen Fool with Wealth: Her Beauty and Merit are lost upon the Dolt, who is insensible of Perfection in any thing. Their Hours together are either painful or insipid" (no. 437). Worse yet is the arrangement by parents of a marriage doomed to such unpleasantness; as one unhappy suitor, a correspondent to the *Spectator,* found to his dismay, some parents calculate the value of an estate and equate that with a son's or daughter's future happiness: "I owe my being at first received to a Comparison of my Estate with that of a former Lover, and that I am now in like Manner turned off, to give Way to an humble Servant still richer than I am" (no. 310). Indeed, "mercenary Motives for making Alliances" can bring lifetimes of unhappiness, both for those who marry for love of wealth, as does Tristissa (no. 326), and for those who fail to marry in a greedy search for the wealthiest suitor, as do the three sisters who pride themselves on their relatives' money (no. 282).[15]

Steele's awareness of the manifold problems with the institution of marriage did not make him a cynic about the potential for happiness in the married state. In fact, his often-voiced interest in the obstacles to marital happiness suggests his belief in the possibility of happiness and contentment within marriage, if a man and a woman join with a true interest in each other and without the constraint of other parties. Steele praises marriage as the source of humankind's highest happiness on earth, realizing, of course, that such delight can be turned to misery and despair. But Steele's hope and trust persevere, as he proclaims: "Marriage is an Institution calculated for a constant Scene of as much Delight as our Being is capable of. Two Persons who have chosen each other out of all the Species, with Design to be each other's mutual Comfort and Entertainment, have in that Action bound themselves to be good-humour'd, affable, discreet, forgiving, patient, and joyful, with Respect to each other's Frailties and Perfections, to the End of their Lives" (no. 490). One notes the emphasis Steele places on affective and emotional qualities, to the surprising subordination of intellectual abilities; for Steele, these exemplary emotional qualities indicate a sensitive and benevolent personality, akin to Bevil, Jr., and Indiana in *The Conscious Lovers.* With a proper approach to and understanding of marriage, says Steele, recommending "always a Disposition to be pleased," people have an excellent opportunity for happiness.

Most of his advice is applicable to both husbands and wives, but it is interesting to observe a slightly greater emphasis upon husbands' treatment of wives. Steele is by no means ignoring women or their difficulties in contemporary life; in fact, he is quick to blame husbands for marital unhappiness: "I have hardly ever observed the married Condition unhappy, but from want of Judgment or Temper in the Man" (no. 479). Though not a feminist according to modern standards, Steele readily acknowledges that much marital unhappiness derives from customs of courtship and marriage contracts largely controlled by men. He urges men to examine their lives for areas of possible improvement, including the treatment of their wives: "I have very long entertained an Ambition to make the Word *Wife* the most agreeable and delightful Name in Nature" (no. 490). Steele's bias is beyond doubt—the family milieu provides greater satisfaction than the fashionable atmosphere of the town, when it is based on mutual love and respect.[16] Though he may not have been a homebody, Steele certainly believed in "the family man."

In promulgating his positive view of marriage, Steele offered examples of marriages made for the right reasons, as he perceived them. In *Spectator* 278, a female correspondent, Florinda, describes her dilemma in choosing a husband: is money or love of paramount importance? Throughout her letter she recognizes the importance her relations place on a prudent (financially beneficial) marriage connection, yet she also knows that her life and her happiness are at stake. She insists that Mr. Spectator advise her whether to listen to the voice of worldly interest or to the voice of her heart recommending her suitor's merit and regard. The habitual reader knows Mr. Spectator's answer before the letter is completed, and so too does Florinda. She has followed her heart and married already. Mr. Spectator's approbation requires no comment. Another letter, from Mary Home, reenforces this perception of marriage as a union designed for happiness and comfort. Mary Home writes to her former friend, Lydia, who has enjoyed some flippant sarcasm about marriage and retirement away from London; Lydia says, "[T]o be marry'd I find is to be bury'd alive," but Mary replies with overwhelming earnestness that she indeed is happy with her husband and her life in the country: "I am marry'd, and have no other concern but to please the Man I love" (no. 254). Mary strikes a devastating blow at the conclusion of her letter, warning that today's fine ladies and coxcombs shall soon be ridiculous in old age. Another letter looks at marriage from the perspective of old age, this one from a dying woman to her soldier-husband away in Spain. Written in a serious, pathetic vein, the letter reviews the comfort and mutual dedication their marriage has afforded: "I pass away my last Hours in Reflection upon the Happiness we have lived in together, and in Sorrow that it is so soon to have an End" (no. 204). This letter, printed undoubtedly with Steele's approbation, nullifies the often-repeated joking about the desirability of widowhood echoed throughout Restoration comedy. In addition, the letter's emotional fervor demonstrates that love does not necessarily disappear in the early years of marriage, leaving only the empty shell of a relationship; indeed, it suggests what Steele has been teaching all along, that marriage can be a source of lifelong felicity and contentment.

The Characters of Women

Steele appropriated considerable space in the *Spectator* to discussions for and about women. His ideas about the proper roles for women are relatively clear and traditional, whereas his perception of women's intellectual capabilities is more advanced than the degrading attitudes of many of his contemporaries. Steele does not ever appear to have doubted the rightness of his prescribing models of behavior for women, as well as severe criticism for those who depart from his ideals. His perceptions of women's roles in English society apparently corresponded with the ideas of his readers, for these discussions did not hurt the popularity of the *Spectator*. To make his points, he often uses characters and short stories as particular examples of his precepts; the stories offer both exemplary characters for imitation and erring characters for ridicule and avoidance.[17] Steele's highest approbation attends the domestic virtues, especially good nature, wit, and humor, and his strongest disapproval is reserved for artificiality and what might be called sophistication.

To praise a woman's good nature, believes Steele, is to applaud her positive attitude toward her family, her neighbors, and her life. Good nature is far more important than beauty because it is both longer lasting and constantly beneficial to those it touches. To the woman who regrets the loss of her beauty through small-pox, Mr. Spectator replies that she may actually have received a benefit: her suitors will now desire her for lasting qualities of mind and not for a passing beauty of face. His advice must have warmed the heart of many a plain wife in England, as he announces the unhappy fate of men married to beautiful women: "Ask any of the Husbands of your great Beauties, and they'll tell you that they hate their Wives Nine Hours of every Day they pass together" (no. 306). Together with his praise of good nature in women is naturally joined his high regard for women's intellectual capabilities, thought by some male contemporaries to be inferior to men's. Steele believes that intellectural activity and the pursuit of knowledge will draw women away from petty gossip, envy, affectation, and other ills which fill empty minds. He recommends reading and approaches, at least, a belief in the intellectual equality of men and women, in a supposed letter from Annabella: "Your directing us to Reading is certainly the best Means to our Instruction. . . [;] we are not generally so Ignorant as Ill-taught. . . [;] our Sex does [not] so often want Wit, Judgment, or Knowledge, as the right application of them" (no. 95). One might not consider this attitude radical, and yet for its day it was certainly advanced. Steele saw women as human beings capable of rational activity, not mere objects for men's use, and this is the essence of his argument throughout the *Spectator*. At the same time, however, he believed that women should fulfill a definite role without complaint—the role of wife and mother. Steele's dictum on this issue is surprisingly resolute and dogmatic: "the utmost of a Woman's Character is contained in Domestick Life . . . . All she has to do in this World is contained within the Duties of a Daughter, a Sister, a Wife, and a Mother" (no. 342). [18] Women belong unquestionably, according to Mr. Spectator's view of the world, in the domestic sphere. Thus Steele's perception of women is eclectic, advanced in his respect for women's intellectual potential and yet strongly traditional in limiting women to nothing more than a domestic, household life.

His criticism of women's ill behavior derives, of course, from his positive expectations of women. Those who misuse or ignore their abilities, who live only in shallowness and affectation, or who disdain the domestic role receive his sharp, satiric reprimand. Those women, such as Mary Astell and others, who attempted to develop societies of women outside the rule of men were awarded the nickname of Platonic ladies and the thoroughgoing scorn of Richard Steele. Unfortunately, he turns to mockery rather than to reasonable discourse, suggesting that these Platonic ladies are after all only hypocrites who are hiding their sexual frailties under a specious system. I have "but a low Opinion of Platonick Love," says Mr. Spectator, "For which Reason I thought it necessary to give my fair Readers a Caution against it, having, to my great Concern, observed the Waste of a Platonist lately swell to a Roundness which is inconsistent with that Philosophy" (no. 400). His anger falls as well upon those who in any way endanger or disturb domestic tranquillity. Among these are coquettes who enjoy tormenting their male admirers and gossips who live by spreading malicious reports of otherwise happy people. Of these, the coquette may distract, but the malicious may destroy, and is therefore the greater danger, ruining for others that which is of no value to her and which she could not gain.[19] The potential for evil in women is great, implies Steele, especially when the passions, such as jealousy, anger, vanity, or hatred, overwhelm reason.

The characters that exemplify the multitude of positive and negative female traits are an ingenious achievement; even though they are types, they come alive upon the page. Perhaps the most brilliant creation is Sir Roger's Perverse Widow, but there are other, shorter character sketches that are almost equally effective. Among these is the story of Laetitia and Daphne, illustrating Steele's belief that the plain but good-natured woman makes a far better wife than does a beautiful but disagreeable lady. Laetitia is proud of her beauty and enjoys making slaves of her admirers, whereas Daphne is a thoughtful, cheerful, and companionable person (nos. 33, 53). The wealthy suitor of the story, after observing both sisters a while, has the good sense to prefer Daphne, and Steele cannot help expressing his delight: "I do not know any thing that has pleased me so much a great while" (no. 33). While Daphne appeals because of her humility, another positive character, Fidelia, appeals because of her unselfish domesticity as she attends her aged, ailing father. "How have I been charmed to see one of the most beauteous Women the Age has produced on her Knees helping on an old Man's Slipper," says Mr. Spectator, and it is apparent that the pathos of this scene—the sacrifice of Fidelia's inclinations to her father's needs—is designed to charm readers as well. The unquestioned assumption is that Fidelia's dutiful domesticity is the correct moral choice. Yet another model which Steele presents in his short fiction is Statira, a woman of good sense and good nature, whose "Features are enlivened with the Chearfulness of her Mind, and [whose] good Humour gives an Alacrity to her eyes" (no. 41). Statira reconfirms Steele's emphasis on good nature as the essential quality to be sought in women. Statira is opposed to women whom he calls Picts, a group identified by their use of much cream and powder on their faces. These are the painted ones—unnatural, Steele might say—and they were a jest for many essayists and dramatists from the Restoration onward.[20]

The moral problem with the Picts, as Steele views them, lies in their seeking approval from society through their appearance, when instead they should—as Steele's ideal women do—seek the approval of their own consciences through their deeds. Because of this flaw of character, Honoria, Flavia, Brunetta, and Phillis become objects of Steele's satire (nos. 91, 80). Honoria and Flavia are mother and daughter in competition for society's admiration; instead of complementing each other, they willingly diminish each other in the eyes of the world. A true sense of worth, suggests Steele, must come from within, not from the fickle and biased opinion of the world, and it must be based not on the temporary attractions of appearance but on the more lasting qualities of good sense and good nature.

The Characters of Men

Steele is above all a practical moralist, for it was apparently his pleasure to analyze human character. He examines male characters both in the abstract and through example, dividing the wide variety of traits into the commendable and the reprehensible. He appears quite comfortable with the role of moral censor, as he was in the *Tatler;* he has little difficulty prescribing moral choices. Most of his advice, even his penchant for satirizing henpecked husbands, comes as no surprise to a reader familiar with the Steele of *The Christian Hero* and *The Conscious Lovers.*

One might argue that a henpecked husband is a problem of manners rather than morals, but for Steele it was definitely a breach of moral order worthy of satire. One of his cardinal beliefs is that a woman's proper place is in the home, and a natural corollary is that a husband must be the domestic leader of the family. The husband who is ruled by his wife—as is the case with Nathaniel Henroost in *Spectator* 176—is assisting in the subversion of domestic order. Steele returns to the subject surprisingly often, usually with good-natured but pointed satire. The letter from Nathaniel Henroost is an appeal to Mr. Spectator for a defense "in Behalf of the Hen-peckt in general." Henroost invokes Socrates as an authority, suggesting "his philosophick Resignation to his Wife Xantippe," and he declares that "the Wise and Valiant in all Ages have been hen-peckt." Unfortunately, his wife sees him writing, and, although he has much more to say, he decides to seal his letter immediately. To this letter Steele opposes a letter from Anthony Freeman, who plans to defy his wife and no longer be—he claims—henpecked. The tone of this letter is more serious and more desperate; Steele allows the letter to stand without comment, permitting readers to draw their own conclusions (no. 212). A following letter from Tom Meggot, Freeman's friend, describes the scene as Freeman attempts to exercise his will independently of his wife; it is a scene worthy of the stage, with Freeman indecisive, Mrs. Freeman railing, and Tom scalded by hot tea (no. 216). Steele is at his best in these depictions of henpecked distress, for he is able to mingle humor with his lesson. When he turns to precept, he often becomes overly serious and much less affable as, for example, at the conclusion of *Spectator* 510: "The old Argument, that 'You do not love me if you deny me this,' which first was used to obtain a Trifle, by habitual Success will oblige the unhappy Man who gives Way to it, to resign the Cause even of his Country and his Honour."[21] This theme recurs frequently in the *Spectator*.

Male behavior in early eighteenth-century England certainly called for commentary on more than henpecked husbands. One of the more unusual phenomena of the period was the Mohocks, a group of wealthy young men who enjoyed the role of a roving, lawless gang of midnight robbers. The Mohocks received a great deal of publicity for their nighttime revels, even having a play by John Gay named after them. Steele described through letters the unpleasantness of dealing with this unorganized gang, whom some thought were instigated by Tories and others by Whigs: "In this Manner they carry on a War against Mankind; and by standing Maxims of their Policy, are to enter into no Alliances but one, and that is offensive and defensive with all Bawdy-Houses in general, of which they have declar'd themselves Protectors and Guarantees" (no. 324). A letter in which Jack Lightfoot describes with humor the dilemma of those caught in a "sweat" by the Mohocks (no. 332) helps Steele to alert the populace to the danger and yet to ridicule the Mohocks out of their vaunted power.

Although the Mohocks were a threat, their alienation from society affected a relatively small number of people. In contrast, the common faults endemic to the Englishmen of the time were of more interest to Steele and of greater applicability to the *Spectator*'s readers. Steele collected a variety of male oddities and gave them generic titles, such as friblers, meddlers, castle-builders, and male jilts. Indeed, he appears to have enjoyed dissecting these jovially satirized faults, reflecting upon both manners and morals. Most of Steele's didactic emphasis, however, falls upon the correction of moral faults; for idiosyncrasies in manners and modes of life he shows tolerance and sometimes appreciation.

In general, his criticism falls upon those who fail to deal with life in a practical, forthright way and who fail to deal with people in an honest, benevolent manner. He offers a mild censure of meddlers, "Persons, who for want of something to do, out of a certain Vacancy of Thought, rather than Curiosity, are ever meddling with things for which they are unfit" (no. 43). The problem with these men lies not in their interest in public affairs, but in their substitution of talk for action. By attending only to affairs about which they can do nothing, they ignore or forget real problems on their level. Such men have undoubtedly lived in all times and places, and Steele's didactic intent may very well be applicable today. The satire applies to many of the *Spectator*'s readers, as well as to Mr. Spectator himself: "One may see now and then this Humour accompanied with an insatiable Desire of knowing what passes, without turning it to any Use in the World but meerly their own Entertainment" (no. 228).

Worse than these talkative fellows are those men who are careless with fact and truth. These people construct in their imaginations what they do not find in the real world. One correspondent writes to Mr. Spectator, "If you think fit we might be called *The Historians,* for *Liar* is become a very harsh Word. . . [;] an Historian, in Conversation, is only a Person of so pregnant a Fancy that he cannot be contented with ordinary Occurrences" (no. 136). In *Spectator* 167 Steele refers to them as castle-builders; they are the Walter Mittys of the eighteenth century who constructed castles in the air. "A Castle-Builder is even just what he pleases," says Mr. Spectator's wide-eyed correspondent, but to Steele and to most of his readers he provided an example of "the unhappy Force of an Imagination unguided by the Check of Reason and Judgment" (no. 167). Another example, more serious because it touches the lives of others, is the heedless promiser, who makes commitments without any intention of keeping them. All of these men, in one way or another, fail to maintain credibility with themselves and with their neighbors.

Worse yet are a group of men whom Steele calls friblers or male jilts, who like heedless promisers fail to keep their word. "A Fribler is one who professes Rapture and Admiration for the Woman to whom he addresses, and dreads nothing so much as her Consent. His Heart can flutter by the Force of Imagination; but cannot fix from the Force of Judgment," says Mr. Spectator with contempt. Friblers and male jilts cause as much unhappiness as coquettes, but they may be more pernicious because they have more power in courtship. There is in the nature of these men both an indecisiveness which makes them weak and a desire for control over others. Steele illustrates the varieties of thoughtlessness, unkindness, and selfishness which detract from good nature and good sense. He always has praise for the "portable quality of good Humour," and his advice to all those whom his satire has touched to the quick—to all of his readers for that matter—is "that it is Prudence to preserve a Disposition in our selves to receive a certain Delight in all we hear and see" (no. 100).

This essentially positive approach to life Steele incorporates in his ideal man—the fine gentleman—who is characterized by heroic courage and fortitude, gentle benevolence, strong emotions, sexual restraint before marriage, filial respect, and a powerful sense of virtue.[22] "In a word, to be a Fine Gentleman, is to be a Generous and a Brave Man" (no. 75). Through various incidents and experiences, Steele emphasizes generous benevolence as a primary trait of a good man. The desire to wish one's friends well arises from emotions channeled to virtue by reason and religion. Steele emphasizes the religious and emotional aspects of benevolence in *Spectator* 248: "Such Natures one may call Stores of Providence, which are actuated by a secret celestial Influence to undervalue the ordinary Gratifications of Wealth, to give Comfort to an Heart loaded with Affliction, to save a falling Family, to preserve a Branch of Trade in their Neighborhood, and give Work to the Industrious, preserve the Portion of the helpless Infant, and raise the Head of the mourning Father." With emotion tempered by good nature and good sense to an enlightened and perspicacious benevolence, the fine gentleman serves as a model for the *Spectator*'s male readers. The personification of Steele's fine gentleman is Bevil, Jr., of *The Conscious Lovers,* who refuses to duel with his friend and at the same time maintains a balanced, benevolent, and reasonable temper.[23]

Steele has praise as well for the man of heroic mind and for soldiers who give generous service to their country. Naturally his experience as a soldier provides material for these reflections, as in *Spectator* 152: "There is no Sort of People whose Conversation is so pleasant as that of military Men, who derive their Courage and Magnanimity from Thought and Reflection. . . [;] no Company can be more amiable than that of Men of Sense who are Soldiers." More pointed, however, is his praise of the most famous soldiers of the day, the Duke of Marlborough and Prince Eugene, who were Whig heroes and leaders in the War of the Spanish Succession.[24] Steele often displays his hero worship of the Duke of Marlborough, whom he calls the "great Officer who foregoes the Advantages he might take to himself, and renounces all prudential Regards to his own Person in Danger" (no. 206). It is likely that, in Steele's mind at least, the Duke of Marlborough displayed the highest qualities of the fine gentleman that Steele so admired.

Parents and Children

Steele's concern with the moral complexities of adult life probably encouraged his interest in the problems of childhood. He, in fact, shows unusual sensitivity for his time, not only to the difficulties of the maturing child but also to the anxieties of parenthood. In his *Spectator* papers he recommends in one way or another that parents be interested in the welfare of their children, from nursing through adolescence and education to marriage and family. His belief in the positive potential of human nature convinced him that young people would grow up to be moral and dependable if given responsive parents and a reasonable education. His disgust with the common practice of corporal punishment as a tool in education grew out of his conviction that true learning is achieved not in fear but through encouragement and interest. Steele focuses in his *Spectator* papers primarily on the parents' responsibility in raising children, and he allows his readers to experience the manifold emotions of parents through his case histories. His message remains constant: parents should demonstrate their care for children by a loving but firm discipline, a keen interest in their education, and responsible guidance in choosing a marriage partner and a career.

Steele shows a strong revulsion to the common practice of farming out a newly born child to a wet nurse: "It is unmerciful to see, that a Woman endowed with all the Perfections and Blessings of Nature, can, as soon as she is delivered, turn off her innocent, tender, and helpless Infant, and give it up to a Woman that is (ten thousand to one) neither in Health nor good Condition" (no. 246). Despite his appeals the practice continued; it was the likely cause of Samuel Johnson's scrofula. Steele argues with highly emotional rhetoric that parents have a responsibility to their child for its well-being: "The Generation of the Infant is the Effect of Desire, but the Care of it argues Virtue and Choice."

The quality of a child's health, both in mind and body, may very well be the result of parents' executing their responsibility in an enlightened and caring manner. In *Spectator* 192 Steele contrasts opposing modes of child rearing and their likely results. Ruricola treated his son with severity and distance rather than freedom and affability, and the result is a son who dislikes not only his father but even his father's mode of life. In contrast appears the family of the Cornelii, "where the Father lives with his Sons like their eldest Brother, and the Sons converse with him as if they did it for no other Reason but that he is the wisest Man of their Acquaintance." Steele's delight in this scene becomes almost extravagant: "It is the most beautiful Object the Eyes of Man can behold, to see a Man of Worth and his Son live in an entire unreserved Correspondence." Perhaps the delight expressed here indicates Steele's sensitivity to the emotional vulnerability of parents. In *Spectator* 263 a father happy with the character of his son describes "the Earnings of Heart, which a Man has when he sees his Child do a laudable thing, or the sudden Damp which seises him when he fears he will act something unworthy." Steele places the highest importance on the emotion of love shared among family members; this is his ideal.

Love, he suggests, is an important component in the education process as well. In *Spectator* 330 he offers contrasting examples of educational experiences for children; in one case a young man had been rescued from poverty and debauchery by a relation, who provided books to study and a great deal of fatherly affection. In a letter to Mr. Spectator, this eighteen-year-old explains his successful reformation: "He has an authority of a Father over me, founded upon the Love of a Brother. . . [;] by this Gentleman's Favour and Patronage, it is my own Fault if I am not wiser and richer every Day I live." The learning of this young man, both from books and from life, is gained from encouragement and comfort, not from threats and punishment. And if this comes from a guardian, how much more responsive should parents be to their offspring. Unfortunately, many parents are completely unresponsive to their children, as in the contrasting letter from a fourteen-year-old boy. With this letter Steele reveals the callous selfishness of a father who begrudges the purchase of books and the cost of a schoolmaster for a son who enjoys studying Latin more than anything else in life. His son claims that he "would chuse rather to be a Scholar, than a Prince without Learning," but his father continues to discourage him from enjoying education. Steele has touched on a relatively common problem, namely, parents who want their children to be or to do the opposite of what the children wish. How much more important is the son's peace of mind and future than this small expense, but the father will only appreciate his mistake after his son has left home—or perhaps when he has read *Spectator* 330.

Even the traditional separate educations for boys and girls, to the undoubted detriment of women's potential intellectual achievement, come under strong criticism. "The general Mistake among us in the educating our Children, is, that in our Daughters we take Care of their Persons and neglect their Minds; in our Sons, we are so intent upon adorning their Minds, that we wholly neglect their Bodies" (no. 66). Steele advocates an intellectually adventurous and exciting learning experience, based on interest rather than fear, for both girls and boys. This was unquestionably a radical proposal at the time, although some progress was being made in women's education.

Steele has definite recommendations on how *not* to raise children as well. His chief objection is to the habitual use of corporal punishment and his second is to fathers who unfeelingly deny their sons reasonable pleasures, a quality education, and parental affection. Steele becomes strongly emotional as he discusses corporal punishment: "I have very often with much Sorrow bewailed the Misfortune of the Children of Great-Britain, when I consider the Ignorance and Undiscerning of the Generality of School-masters" (no. 157). In *Spectator* 168 a correspondent refers to schoolmasters as licensed tyrants, urging Mr. Spectator "to enter the Lists against so many armed Paedagogues." Steele's goal is stated well in that same letter: "We might then possibly see Learning become a Pleasure." Equally displeasing to Steele is the experience of young people who suffer from a father's neglect, avarice, or jealousy (no. 431, 496), and he becomes almost emotionally involved as he attempts to shame and reform those who may be guilty of these faults. Nevertheless, his ideas on child rearing and education were practical and reasonable, though certainly well ahead of their time. Educational theory and practice have taken a long time to catch up with Richard Steele.

Wit and Morality

Steel's emphasis in his *Spectator* papers on moral didacticism is perhaps a hallmark of his work. His intention is beyond doubt: to arouse his readers to a greater awareness and thereby a fuller practice of benevolent morality in day-to-day personal relationships. Addison's announced intention to "enliven Morality with Wit, and to temper Wit with Morality" in *Spectator* 10 was perhaps accepted with less conviction by Steele, for given an opposition between morality and wit Steele would champion the cause of morality. Most of his papers deal in one way or another with advice for apparently realistic moral dilemmas, often through the use of correspondence. In the counsel that he provides, directly or indirectly, Steele usually ranks reason and judgment superior to beauty and wit as guides to virtue; the attainment of virtue, or in other words right moral judgment in action, is a major purpose of life, as Steele perceived it, and the *Spectator* through its ruminations assists toward that goal.[25]

The key to Steele's direction appears early in the *Spectator,* as he indicates his intention to take on as the enemy most of the ill habits of life and to attempt to improve the habitual morality of his readers: "There is hardly that Person to be found, who is not more concern'd for the Reputation of Wit and Sense, than Honesty and Virtue. But this unhappy Affectation of being Wise rather than Honest, Witty than Good-Natur'd, is the Source of most of the ill Habits of Life" (no. 6). But Mr. Spectator becomes discouraged over his distinct lack of progress: "It gives me much Despair in the Design of reforming the World by my Speculations when I find that there always arise from one Generation to another successive Cheats and Bubbles as naturally as Beasts of Prey and those which are to be their Food" (no. 444). If the *Spectator* did not change the course of life for thousands, it may still have touched the lives of readers in a variety of unknown ways. What is more important, as the mutual achievement of Steele and Addison the *Spectator* lives—not as a monument, for that would suggest coldness and death—but as a delightfully readable reflection of the authors' and their society's expectations of life. The *Spectator* is by no means of historical interest only; again and again these essays touch a modern reader with insights that seem as fresh now as they were then. The *Spectator* is not a monument worthy of respect but a perception of life worthy of examination. Mr. Spectator lives.

Chapter Six

Political Struggles Continue: The Later Periodicals

The *Guardian*

Steele turned from the *Spectator* to the *Guardian* in order to alter the emphasis of his periodical writing, consonant with the politically strained relations in 1713. He proposed to venture into political disputes with his new journal, an area generally avoided in his two earlier periodicals. Published daily, except for Sunday, from March 12 to October 1, 1713, *The Guardian* was given an elaborate background of characters and a carefully drawn mask-author, Nestor Ironside. Imitating his namesake's pattern in *The Aeneid*, Nestor is an old man who gives sound advice to his people; indeed he is the guardian of his people, though not their leader.[1] The second part of his name, Ironside, suggests the boldness, courage, and strength of loyal people under siege. Nestor's position within the *Guardian* is analogous to his position as writer of the *Guardian:* within he is the protector of the Lizard family— grandmother, mother, four sons, and five daughters—and as putative author he is counselor and adviser to those who need him. Therein lies Richard Steele's major concern: he perceives the need for a publication to guard the English people against the Tory propaganda in the *Examiner.* The socially oriented papers in the *Guardian* attracted a receptive audience for the political papers. Still, many papers have wit and urbanity much in the style of the *Tatler* and the *Spectator,* with only occasional papers dipping into the morass of political attack and counterattack.

The framework that Steele develops in the *Guardian* is elaborate, and it is interesting because it shows that he is taking seriously the role of Censor of Great Britain which he lightheartedly adopted in the *Tatler*. In the *Guardian* Nestor exerts authority over English people and institutions: "My Design upon the whole is no less, than to make the Pulpit, the Bar, and the Stage, all act in Concert in the Care of Piety, Justice and Virtue."[2] In a small way, but with warm regard and reasonable consideration, Nestor exercises a similar authority over the Lizard family, to which he is advisor and legal guardian. Even the daughters' marriages must have Nestor's as well as My Lady Lizard's approval: "If it were possible for a Man, who had never entered into the State of Marriage, to know the Instincts of a kind Father to an Honourable and Numerous House, I may say I have done it" (no. 5). The family includes five daughters, Jane, Annabella, Cornelia, Betty, and Mary, each exemplifying various female characteristics. Jane is interested in household supervision, in imitation of her mother. Twenty-three and unmarried, she is a likely subject for discussion of marriage. Annabella is a bright but self-centered daughter, a likely subject for discussions of female vanity. Cornelia is the reader of pastorals, while Betty is the gossip. But the youngest, Mary, is his favorite, "the very Quintescence of good Nature and Generosity," whom Nestor has named the Sparkler. These are Nestor Ironside's family, the recipients of his right-minded authority, the model for a more diffuse moral authority over his English readers.

The sons are also subject to Nestor's guidance and authority. Ranging in age from twenty-six to twenty, the four Lizard boys have a variety of interests which require advice and commentary. The eldest, Sir Harry, has his own estate; because he is an eligible bachelor, he receives detailed admonitions from Nestor about the selection of a wife. Nestor even proposes a specific young lady, and when he suspects that Sir Harry is more interested in taking a mistress than a wife, he devotes *Guardian* 68 to a firm warning against ruining a chaste woman of low fortune. Sir Harry, like the Sparkler, is Nestor's favorite, and the advice sent to him serves all young men in the reading audience. The other boys receive less attention, serving more as types in order to introduce discussion topics. Tom, aged twenty-four, is the sportsman, wit, and storyteller; William, with an inquisitive temper and serious outlook, is preparing to study law; while the youngest, John, desires to take holy orders.

As a result of its emphasis on young people and their interests, the *Guardian* offers Steele an excellent opportunity for a discussion of his attitudes toward education. Sir Harry's education is a case in point: Nestor is very proud of Sir Harry's business acumen and mathematical knowledge. "It has been carefully provided in his Education, that he should be very ready at Calculation," says Nestor, so that he will understand the credit and debit accounts on the farms of his estate.[3] Nestor strongly approves the mode of Sir Harry's education as well: instructed by a grammar-master with the other children of the nieghborhood. The social skills gained through this group's educational growth together have gained Sir Harry long-lasting friendships and an easy, congenial manner. In a later *Guardian* essay, No. 94, Nestor provides more specific recommendations about educational methods. Education ought to be tailored to the ability of the student; in other words, Latin and Greek ought not to be taught to an incapable student. Second, tutors ought to be respected and paid well. Nestor asserts that some footmen are paid more than tutors, an inexcusable disrespect for teachers. Third, good sense and good nature are more important than pedantry. These three items, which perhaps seemed radical to many in his day, form a cornerstone in Steele's attitudes toward education, teachers, and students.

More often than not, despite Steele's political intentions, Nestor's guidance turns to manners and morals rather than politics. Nestor recommends businesslike abilities, mildly but repeatedly presenting the need to understand mathematical calculations, to improve an estate, and to reconcile land and trading interests. He analyzes once again the attributes of a fine gentleman and derides the libertine man of mode. He discusses natural and fantastical pleasures, praises the didacticism of *Cato,* and examines the rules of conversation and storytelling. He categorizes laughers, discusses religion and courtship, and praises female chastity;

he also provides an extended discussion of pastoral, possibly by Thomas Tickell, that ultimately causes Steele some embarrassment.[4] These interests appear much in the mode of the *Tatler* and the *Spectator,* with liveliness and wit; indeed, the *Guardian*'s stern image is to some degree undeserved. The entrance of politics, however, tended to diminish the vigor of the *Guardian* papers, and the attacks on the *Examiner* became monotonously repetitive. The fear of anything French, the papers on Dunkirk, and even Nestor's awareness of his own seriousness indicate the increasing political tension during 1713 and hint at Steele's lack of any further desire to entertain topics on manners and morals. Steele continues moving toward a journal primarily political in later *Guardian* papers, and thus it is a natural evolution for Nestor Ironside to turn over his journalistic powers to the more political *Englishman* in October, 1713.

The *Englishman*

Steele saw the *Englishman* as a more serious, more politically oriented continuation of the *Guardian.* Although numerous entertaining papers still appear in the *Englishman,* the emphasis even more than in the *Guardian* falls upon the unrelenting political difficulties in England in 1713. The Whigs were fearful that the Tory ministry would subvert the body of law supporting the Protestant Succession; with Queen Anne's declining health the danger of the Roman Catholic Pretender wielding power in England seemed frightening indeed. The persona for this publication, simply the Englishman himself, is a transparent cover for Steele, although he himself signed three letters to the *Englishman.* Steele makes clear to his readers his concern for the nation's health and stability, as he explains the transition from the *Guardian* to the *Englishman* in the first issue: "For valuable Considerations I have purchased the Lion, Desk, Pen, Ink, and Paper, and all other Goods of Nestor Ironside, Esq; who has thought fit to write no more himself, but has given me full Liberty to report any sage Expressions or Maxims which may tend to the Instruction of Mankind, and the Service of his Country."[5] He explains his intention to move further away from the discussion of manners and mores of the *Spectator* and to devote his energies primarily to politics: "It is not, said the good Man, giving me the Key of the Lion's Den, now a Time to improve the Taste of Men by the Reflections and Railleries of Poets and Philosophers, but to awaken their Understanding, by laying before them the present State of the World like a Man of Experience, and a Patriot." As a result, the *Englishman* has a much more limited interest for twentieth-century readers, as it probably had for eighteenth-century readers as well. The *Englishman* as an occasional paper was out of date for the most part by 1720.

The *Englishman* appeared in two entirely separate issues; the first was published in fifty-seven numbers from October 6, 1713, to February 15, 1714, and was concerned primarily with the Tory ministry's suspected leanings toward the Roman Catholic Pretender while retaining references to an old friend, Nestor Ironside, and to some degree his interest in lessons on manners and morals. The second issue, bleaker and darker in tone, was published after the death of Queen Anne and the accession of King George in order to prove the allegations against the now-ousted Tory government. In the Preface to the second volume of the *Englishman* Steele announces his purpose: "The Former Volume of the *Englishman* was written with a direct Intention to destroy the credit, and frustrate the designs of Wicked Men, at that Time in Power. . . . That Volume alarm'd Mankind against their Designs; and This lays together Facts which must convince all the World of the Methods they had taken to accomplish them." There is very little enjoyment in reading the second volume of the *Englishman,* which appeared in thirty-eight issues from July 11, 1715, to November 21, 1715, a time of tension and fear reflected darkly in its pages. The ominous tone of this publication may be heard in No. 4 of the second volume: "The Posture of our present Affairs cannot but raise the utmost Indignation of every Man who loves either his Country, his Religion, or his Liberty." Calling the Tory ministers *Parricides,* the Englishman claims that they were directly involved in treasonable negotiations with the Pretender and French ministers. "The Breach of Treaties, the Slavery of his Country, and Destruction of all Things which are valuable amongst Men, were not only design'd by this Lord, [Bolingbroke] with propense Malice and Treachery, but also executed with Wantonness and Pleasure" (vol. 2, no. 9). Not surprisingly, this volume of the *Englishman* concluded with a condemnation of those who could straddle the fence and attempt to remain uncommitted. Steele, of course, had committed his life and fortune to the Whig cause, for the good of his country as well as his own hoped-for prosperity. After observing his countrymen's unconcern about the most important issues of the day, he reacts with disgust toward those he believes are indifferent to England's fate: "The Indifferents should be thrown into the Mire, by those who Travel on both Sides of the Way, for pretending the Benefit of the Road, without contributing to the making it either Safe or Good" (vol. 2, no. 38).

The first volume of the *Englishman* is in comparison lighter and more entertaining. Many of its fifty-seven numbers, to be sure, are devoted to attacks on the *Examiner,* the Tory administration, Roman Catholicism, and France; the Treaty of Utrecht and its unfulfilled articles on the destruction of Dunkirk also receive due attention. At the same time, the tone is more hopeful and positive than in the second volume, and the political papers are often interspersed with lighter commentary. The metaphorical call to arms is not to be denied: "A *true Englishman,* in a civil and political Sense, is the greatest Character in Life" (vol. 1, no. 18). A letter from Hannovero-Britannus beats the drums against Popery: "It has been represented as a malicious idle Report, to say, That the Nation is in any present Danger of Popery or the Pretender: and yet it is certain, that the Number of those who have these apprehensions still increases; which would make one suspect that this Danger has been growing every Day more and more visible" (vol. 1, no. 20) Other papers in the *Englishman* (vol. 1), however, return to Nestor Ironside, or discuss the proper method of giving advice, or even tell the story of Alexander Selkirk, the model for Daniel Defoe's Robinson Crusoe (vol. 1, no. 26). The narration of Selkirk's adventures alone on an island is well done, indeed fascinating. Perhaps Defoe also found it fascinating. But the political papers were, of course, primary, and it is clear that the political attack and counterattack amidst continuing abuse took their toll on Richard Steele. Without doubt, though much sadness was yet to come, this must have been a difficult stage in his life. The final paper of the first volume is a long letter signed by Steele, an apologia for his continuing efforts at political propaganda, in which his bitterness finds vent. "I was once so happy in the kind Thoughts of the Generality of People of all Conditions in this Town, that I cannot without Regret look back upon the Loss of it; and indeed I should be still more concerned, had I not forfeited it for such Considerations as only are to be preferred to their good Opinion: all which Considerations I will express in the honest plain Phrase of *the Testimony of a good Conscience*" (vol. 1, no. 57). There is no reason to doubt Steele's unalloyed belief in the moral value of his political writing. Unfortunately, there is no reason to doubt his self-pity either. For all of his work, the fate of England was determined by an accident of history, the sudden death of Queen Anne on August 1, 1714. The Tories were unprepared, George I acceded to the throne, and the Protestant Succession, as Steele had hoped, was safe.

The *Lover*

For the most part, the *Lover* provides a welcome respite from the political wrangling found in Steele's other writing toward the end of Queen Anne's reign. The *Lover* appeared in the spring of 1714, however, a time of increasing political tension for England as well as for Steele, with the threat of the Queen's declining health and the continuing uncertainty of the Protestant Succession. The intensity of Steele's political involvement appears in the acid personal and political satire of the Crabtrees—thoroughly inappropriate in the *Lover;* the Crabtrees represent the family of Sir Robert Harley, the Tory leader and the object here of one of Steele's most virulent attacks. Nevertheless, in most *Lover* papers, the tone is reminiscent of the *Tatler,* with a light, happily eccentric touch to many of the discussions of love and a persona similar in some ways to Isaac Bickerstaff. Steele's authorial mask in the *Lover* is Marmaduke Myrtle, an aging unmarried gentleman who has been transfixed in the passion of love by his constant though unfulfilled devotion to Mrs. Ann Page. This experience, says Mr. Myrtle, "made me place all my Happiness in Hours of Retirement," studying the intricacies and difficulties in the passion of love.[6] Indeed, this dominant passion has caused Myrtle to be oblivious to the practical economic and political concerns of his day, a deficiency that unquestionably separates him from his creator, Richard Steele: "I cannot tell how many Years, Months, Hours, Days or Minutes have passed away since I first saw Mrs. Ann Page; but certain I am, that they have ran by me, without my being much concerned in what was transacted in the World around me all that while."[7] Marmaduke Myrtle appears, then, a quixotic advocate for love as well as a diminished spokesman for a domesticated form of courtly love. At the same time, however, he is an authority on love who resolves dilemmas in courtship and marriage posed by correspondents. Myrtle's position is akin to Dear Abby's, and some of his replies in the *Lover* are remarkably similar to hers. Steele found a comfortable medium in the flow of questions and answers about courtship and marriage, as the relaxed and assured tone of the *Lover* suggests. It is likely that these discussions provided a calm retreat for Steele—as well as for his readers—from the tensions of the day.

At the beginning, the *Lover* is constructed around a club, in a way similar to the *Spectator* (no. 1). The club includes five other gentlemen, most of them less eccentric than Myrtle, who are interested in conversation about love. Two are widowers who seek consolation from this group's discussions, one is a disappointed lover like Myrtle, one is happily married, and the youngest, Mr. Severn, is a sought-after bachelor. The club's conversation, it is implied, will be the subject of many future papers, as Myrtle describes the happily married Mr. Johnson, who "may give Occasion in my future Discourses to draw many Incidents of Domestick Life" (no. 1). The papers did not develop along these lines, however, because among other things Steele turned to his favorite structural device, correspondence. As a result, the *Lover* moved to a dialogue between Myrtle and correspondents, with the epistolary form the model for many of the papers. Ann Page is mentioned often, as is appropriate, for the paper focuses primarily on the solution to love's problems from Marmaduke Myrtle's perspective.

The theory of love underpinning many of the practical and circumstantial discussions is based on Steele's concept of the power of a reformed passion to effect good. His discussion of the power of love in the *Lover* has noteworthy similarities to his analysis of the passions in *The Christian Hero*. In the *Lover* No. 5 Myrtle argues that the passion of love directs man to positive behavior by a general beneficent influence: "When I find in my self so strong an Inclination to oblige and entertain all whom I meet with, accompanied with such a readiness to receive kind impressions of those I converse with, I am more and more convinced that this Passion is in honest Minds the strongest Incentive that can move the Soul of Man to laudable Accomplishments." In the final number Myrtle restates his theory of love to his readers once again, in effect offering a capstone to some of his more didactic papers: "The Bosom into which Love enters, enclines the Person who is inspired with it, with a Goodness towards all with whom he converses, more extensive than even that which is instilled by Charity. I pretend to so much of this noble Passion, as seldom to overlook the Excellencies of other Men" (no. 40). In both of these statements Steele retains the anti-rationalistic belief in the necessity of reformed passions for the achievement of virtue which he expressed thirteen years earlier in *The Christian Hero*: "By this Force of their Make, Men are insensibly hurried into each other, and by a secret Charm we lament with the unfortunate, and rejoice with the Glad; for it is not possible for an human Heart to be averse to any thing that is Human . . . for one Man's Eyes are Spectacles to another to Read his Heart . . . [;] when the Heart is full, [the eyes] will brighten into Gladness, and gush into Tears."[8] The theory here expressed bridges Steele's work from *The Christian Hero* through the *Lover* in 1714 to *The Conscious Lovers* in 1722; in all of these his theme is consistent: it is not possible for a human heart to be averse to anything human. In *The Christian Hero* Steele emphasized tears as an emblem of redeemed passions, at the same time describing the action of the

redeemed passions as universal benevolence, very much in the
form of the command to "Love thy Neighbor": "From this Foundation in nature is kindled that noble Spark of Coelestial Fire,
we call Charity or Compassion, which opens our Bosoms, and
extends our Arms to Embrace all Mankind." The drive to virtue
instigated by the reformed passions, especially the universal passion of love, directs human nature to a "vertuous Enjoyment of
our Passions" as well as to beneficence, according to Steele's
theory. This theory provides the foundation for Marmaduke Myrtle's recommendations about personal relationships—solutions
to love-related problems—to his correspondents.

Myrtle's advice to a correspondent aptly named Charles Doubt
is typical of his practical admonitions to those deciding on marriage. In his letter to Myrtle, Charles writes that he is attracted
to two sisters; Celia he loves for her "agreeable easie Conversation
and Good-humour" and Lucinda he admires because she is "very
handsome, and excellently well shaped" (no. 19). In his advice
Myrtle stresses the more permanent qualities of character over the
more evanescent qualities of appearance: "Celia will gain Ground
of Lucinda; for Beauty palls by intimate Conversation; but good
Humour and Affability gain new Strength the more frequently
they discover themselves." In order for the reformed passion of
love to achieve its objective of guiding and enforcing benevolent
responses, the object of love must be worthy and permanent;
qualities of character are worth one's esteem, while appearance
which is mutable may temporarily attract but is not the worthy
object of sustained love. For Charles Doubt to exemplify Steele's
theory, he must choose Celia rather than Lucinda.

After describing the often unhappy choices of women preparing
for marriage, Myrtle advises his female readers to make their own
decisions and judge suitors themselves, relying for guidance on
permanent qualities of character rather than on appearance,
money, or position. Myrtle strongly discourages the uncritical
acceptance of others' advice in determining a choice in marriage;
for the passion of love to achieve its positive effect, the beloved
must be chosen with complete freedom and for appropriate reasons. Women who are forced or cajoled into marriage have little

opportunity to achieve the full happiness of a dynamic love. Myrtle urges women to think for themselves: "It is the Unhappiness of too many Women of Fortune and Merit (from a distrust of their own Judgment) to submit themselves entirely to the Direction of others" (no. 37). The value of a happy marriage is incalculable, he suggests, especially for women, constrained as they are from other modes of living. Still Myrtle sees marriage in an extraordinarily positive perspective: "A generous and constant Passion, in an agreeable Lover, is the greatest Blessing that can happen to the most deserving of her Sex" (no. 37). One cannot help wondering about the reaction of his female readers to this declaration.

Many other stories in the *Lover* are devoted to depicting and reinforcing the extreme importance of the marriage bond. Steele appears to enjoy the rather strongly emotional tone of these tales, as many of his readers probably did. The most sentimental of them occurs in the *Lover* No. 8, where Myrtle prints correspondence between a wife and her husband on the night before his condemnation and death, with the comment that "I never read anything which, to me, had so much Nature and Love." The letters are in design both public and didactic, rather than personal and intimate, in order to stir the emotions of his readers. The husband proclaims "that Virtue in which we have mutually supported each other," and his wife wishes for her own "Dissolution with you, that so we may go Hand in Hand to Heaven." The tone here reflects less wit and light and more overwhelming and painful sentiment, the consequence perhaps of a change in Steele or his audience. Nevertheless, in the same paper the importance of love as a guiding passion is again reaffirmed, with readers of both sexes directed to be serious and astute in choosing a marriage partner.[9]

Other emotional scenes, some more restrained than others, focus on the death of a wife, with discussions on the acceptance of grief and loss. In the *Lover* No. 26 a selection from *Of Contentment, Patience, and Resignation to the Will of God, in several Sermons* by Isaac Barrow, is prefaced by a correspondent, who says "that it is impossible to read what he has said on this Subject

without being the better for it." R. B., the correspondent, claims
that, after the death of his wife, he sought reading which might
"tend to my Relief under this my great Calamity." Marmaduke
Myrtle prints a considerable quotation and concludes by praising
Barrow, who "had a most inexhaustible Fund of Observation and
good Sense," and by praising a new edition of Barrow's works.
Shortly thereafter Myrtle returns to an extended quotation for the
Lover No. 29; he visits a club member, the widower Mr. Oswald,
who is discovered by Myrtle reading for his consolation *Contem-
plations Moral and Divine* by Sir Matthew Hale, a book used and
written in by Oswald's deceased wife. Mr. Oswald's commentary
provides a frame for quotations from Hale's book, but with considerable emotional impact: "In order to give you a Notion of
her Merit and good Sense, pray give me leave to read three or
four Paragraphs which she has marked with this Pencil. He here
looked upon the Pencil, till the Memory of some little Incident,
of which it reminded him, filled his Eyes with Tears." Steele
prepares for an unqualified acceptance of Hale's religious commentary by touching the emotionally receptive reader with this
pathetic scene. His didactic goal remains the same: to inculcate
a respect for passions reformed by reason and religion which
operate as guides to vitue and benevolence. In the concluding
comments of this paper he offers his readers an abbreviated summary of the human psychology presented in *The Christian Hero.*
At first he suggests that "nothing can mend the Heart better
than an honourable Love, except Religion. It sweetens Disasters,
and moderates good Fortune, from a Benevolent Spirit that is
naturally in it." Shortly thereafter he recommends marriage as
one experience, among others, which may help "to promote that
Delight by all the methods which Reason, urged by Religion and
Duty, forwarded by Passion, can intimate to the Heart." Steele's
perception of human psychology had apparently changed little
over the intervening thirteen years; he continued to accept the
possibility of improved human conduct, not through ameliorated
human nature, but through the combined efforts of human reason
and divine religion.

A different kind of sentimental tale occurs in the story of the Maryland slaves, superficially similar to the Inkle and Yarico story in the *Spectator* but designed to inculcate reverence for the marriage bond. In the *Lover* No. 36 Myrtle tells a story of adultery among a husband, wife, and the husband's best friend, all slaves on a Maryland plantation. The purpose of the story is, as he says, to demonstrate that "even the most Barbarous have regarded adultery with the utmost Horror and Detestation." The story is very simple: while the husband is hunting, the friend seduces his wife and is then discovered by the husband. Rebuking his friend as a traitor, the husband contemplates suicide but is prevented by his remorseful friend, who then resolves to die for the injury done to the husband and wife. Myrtle's witty commentary at the conclusion of the story reveals his estimate of upper-class marriage and fidelity: "If the Wretches of the Nation, who set up for Men of Wit and Gallantry, were capable of feeling the generous Remorse of this poor Slave, upon the like Occasions, we should, I fear, have a much thinner Appearance of Equipage in Town."

If Myrtle displays his wit adeptly with this story, he unfortunately loses his wit and perhaps his wits as he recounts the history of the Crabtree family, a transparent vilification of Robert Harley, the leader of the Tory government, and his relations. Steele felt abused by Harley, and his reaction was to abuse and vilify in return. The Crabtree papers in the *Lover* make unpleasant reading at best, and even Marmaduke Myrtle admits that he is "a little tired with such Ideas" (no. 27) as the satiric attacks on Harley and his family. A few weeks earlier his feeling was much more aggressive, as a fictional correspondent reminded the world that "all these Fellows were bred Presbyterians, and are now set up for High Churchmen" (no. 11). Steele wanted his audience to believe that the Harleys' religious alignment showed that they were driven by political winds and that they were indeed creatures of no integrity: "There is a difference between those who are of neither side, from generous Principles, and those who are disinterested only from having no Principles at all." The lack of religious principles, suggests Steele, reveals a lack of ethical principles entirely, and he accuses Harley of virtually dictatorial measures. "Thus they take upon them to manage all things in this Country; and if any Man is to be Accused, Arrested, or Disgraced, one of these hideous Creatures has certainly a Hand in it." The insistence on Harley's lack of principles continues in the *Lover* no. 14, wherein another presumably fictional correspondent, Ephraim Castlesoap, derides the whole Harley family: "They having as little Respect for Mankind, as Mankind has for them, they do not care how gross the thing is they attempt, so they can carry it." Unfortunately, Steele knows no limits in his mud-slinging against Harley, and he begins to lose control of his temper in the *Lover* no. 16, in which a correspondent—undoubtedly a reference to Steele—who signed himself, "the most unfortunate of Lovers, Ricardo Languenti" makes a vague analogy between Peter in Swift's *A Tale of a Tub* and Sir Anthony Crabtree. Ricardo advises Myrtle to publish his letter against Harley on April Fool's Day, a "Day auspicious to the Crabtrees," and indeed no. 16 is dated Thursday, April 1, 1714. In the final attack upon Harley in the *Lover,* twelve days later, Steele uses another correspondent to complain publicly, perhaps to Harley directly in a cry for attention or perhaps to readers as a warning, that "it is the Nature of the Crabtrees to be blind to the Evils they themselves commit" (no. 21). In any case, with this number the vilification of Harley ends, and the *Lover* returns to a more amiable tone and content. In all, the *Lover* is a remarkably interesting publication, and it is surprising that it has been so thoroughly forgotten. Sections of it certainly rival the *Tatler* in quality.

The *Reader*

At the same time that he was writing the *Lover,* Steele was at work on another periodical named the *Reader*. Whereas the *Lover* is predominantly a non-political, good-humored paper, the *Reader* is almost wholly political. The *Lover* appeared on Tuesday, Thursday, and Saturday from February 25, 1714, to May 27, 1714; the *Reader,* published usually on Monday, Wednesday, and Friday, ran from April 22, 1714, until May 10, 1714, ending with the ninth paper on a bitter note of discouragement and despair: "I can only say with Mr. Bays, *I'll write no more*" (no. 9). Steele must have felt that he had failed in his political pamphleteering for the Whigs; little did he know that victory for the Whigs and the Protestant Succession was less than three months away. The tone of much of the *Reader* is negative and defeatist, perhaps reflecting Steele's own perception of Whig fortunes. Even the shadowy persona, the reader of papers at coffeehouses, proclaims his disenchantment with other papers, alluding no doubt to the *Examiner*'s Tory propaganda and a biased journalism in general.[10] But this reader is difficult to please; he is even unhappy with the coffee. The tone of these papers approximates the tone of the Crabtree papers in the *Lover*. Steele begins in the first paper, April 22, to attack Harley once again, suggesting that he is allied to the French, a new convert who is a dupe of Popery. His intimations about Harley's loyalty are distasteful: "Some Entymologists and Heralds say, the illustrious Names of *Harlay, d'Harcourt,* and *St. Jean,* are originally French." Matters had taken such a turn that in London, in the chancel of the Church of White-Chappel, an altar painting was constructed in which a Whig clergyman, in a priest's gown and band, is represented as Judas."[11]

The political tension of the time even enveloped an otherwise innocuous issue, the invitation to George, Duke of Cambridge and potential successor to the English throne to travel from Hanover in order to visit England. It becomes apparent that Whig partisans expected an invasion of England by the Pretender supported by French money and forces and that the Whigs believed the Tories would show little resistance to such an invasion. Hesitation to invite George to England suggested to paranoid Whigs an alliance of the Tory government with the Pretender. Steele expresses the fears of many Whigs in *Reader* No. 2: "Tho' the Arrival of the Duke of Cambridge would not demolish *Dunkirk,* yet it would make us less fearful of the ill Consequences from its being undemolished; one of which may be an Attempt of imposing upon us the Pretender, whose Invasion would be less dreaded, when one who is a Prince of the Blood was ready to fight against him." The same fear and tension that urged the

Whigs to invite George from Hanover drove Steele to write under cover of allegory, or through ironic satire or nonsense.

The spirit of mystery and intrigue must have been pervasive, present as it is in the *Reader*. Steele feels compelled to imply accusations and to hint sedition: "For when they give up all Rules of Honour and Conscience to hurt and betray the Liberties of Mankind, I shall sacrifice smaller Considerations, and venture now and then to write Nonsense for the Good of my Country . . ." (no. 4). In his next paper Steele's persona, the reader, follows this mysterious proclamation with an ironic letter to the Sword-Bearer of London, who is called upon to cut off the head of the Pretender when he invades London. To write such silly stuff Steele must have felt threatened by the danger of the Pretender's invasion and by the apparent unwillingness of the Tory government to take preventive measures. The words "traitor" and "sedition" are bandied about freely in the arguments with the *Examiner,* and Steele sensed the need to defend publicly himself and Robert Walpole, the future Whig Prime Minister, from recent attacks in the Tory press. Walpole had been attacked as Bullymandra, and Steele defended him courageously, gaining a patron who would be very powerful and helpful seven years later, after the South Sea scandal and Steele's theater patent difficulties.

Steele presses the attack in *Reader* No. 7, wherein he discredits the arguments and information in the *Examiner* and the *Monitor,* both Tory publications. In No. 7 he accuses the *Examiner* of lies, distortion, and prejudice designed to damage the country while promoting the power of the Tories: "The professed, or at least apparent, Design of this Author since he first began, has been to villifie an Administration which rendered the Kingdom of England the Terror of its Enemies and the Refuge of its Friends; and he has done as much in this good Work as the Cause would bear." Steele then writes his attack upon the author of the *Examiner* with mockery of Harley as a New Convert, converted from Dissenter to orthodox Anglican, for, as Steele would suggest, political opportunism. The ironic satire is bitter, probably with Steele's own feelings of anger and hurt, and possibly with genuine displeasure at the Tories' treatment of the Duke of Marlborough.

Steele controls his satiric attack effectively: "Let no one therefore take an Injury that's done him by a Saint, or New Convert, to proceed from Ill-Will. How could a sanctified Person lay a greater Obligation upon another, than by being the Instrument of begetting in him the Virtue of Patience? Suppose a Soldier should have passed through ten Campaigns under a Commander that had reduced his Heart to the Love of the vain Pomps and Vanities of this World, by leading him through a continual Scene of Triumph, what could a new Convert do for him better than to send him a starving?" Steele undoubtedly felt that he and the Whigs were starving in the spring of 1714. After the Whig triumph and the accession of George I with the accompanying spectacular prosperity of many Whig partisans, Steele continued to feel—with good reason—as if he were starving. His unreserved commitment to the Whig cause through the lean Tory years earned him little solid compensation and less gratitude. If he had known the future, it is doubtful that he would have spent his energies so generously for the Whigs as he did.

Evidence of Steele's sense of humor is rare in the *Reader,* but when it does appear, as in no. 8, it is with unabated vigor. Steele's wit and humor make the eighth paper uniquely readable and enjoyable despite its ultimate satiric attack on the Pretender, Popery, and everything French. Steele presents a symbolic tale about English wine and French wine from a correspondent named Ruburb Hearty, comparing the qualities of port wine with French claret. After identifying the English characteristics of moderation, discretion, and reasonableness with port and the French characteristics of gaiety, pleasantry, and exhilaration with claret, the *Reader's* correspondent concludes with a rousing call for English health and a condemnation of the French and their wine: "I have heard a very experienced Vintner say, That he had observed great Difference between the Tempers of his Claret and Port-Customers. The old age of the Claret-Drinker is generally peevish and fretful; that of him who uses Port calm, and at the worst dull. The Blood of a Claret-Drinker grows Vinegar, that of your Port-man Mum. The Effect of Claret is to make Men restless, of Port to make them sleepy. But Port, moderately used, had all the good Effects which can come from the best Claret, and none of the ill Effects which flow from the immoderate Use of it self." The playfulness still appearing through the seriousness of this story suggests that Steele retained his wit and liveliness at least in some form in the midst of terribly depressing times.

Town-Talk, Chit-Chat, and The Theatre

One might easily be misled by the titles of two of these publications, *Town-Talk, in a Letter to a Lady in the Country* and *Chit-Chat, in a Letter to a Lady in the Country,* which sound light, frothy, and gossip-oriented. Both are a far cry from conversational pleasantries. *Town-Talk* is a pamphlet which appeared in nine numbers from December 17, 1715, to February 13, 1716, with the design of improving the stage.[12] Steele had been appointed Governor of the Royal Company of Comedians at Drury Lane Theatre in October, 1714, shortly after the accession of George I and the rise to power of the Whigs. The King's Patent specifically urged the reformation of the stage by the new Governor: "The Reformation of the Stage proposed by the Said Richard Steele is very desirable for the Sake of Religion and good Manners, and, if effected will very much tend to the Honour of Our Government."[13] Steele had promised to reform the stage, and *Town-Talk* was one of his efforts toward that end. Steele, however, although effective as a reformer of the stage both in *The Conscious Lovers* and in the *Spectator,* met with little success through his tenure as Governor of Drury Lane. He began with some assurance in the first issue of *Town-Talk,* after relating a rather bawdy story, to proclaim the change that was to transform Drury Lane: "But they tell us we are to have a mighty amendment in Theatrical Entertainments; for there is, forsooth, a Patent that enables the Undertaker at the House of *Drury-Lane,* to Chastise the Vices of the Stage, and promote the Interests of Virtue and Innocence." An undertaker is akin to an entrepreneur or projector, and it is likely that Steele saw himself as a projector in his attempt to moralize the stage. Like his other projects, his attempt to reform Drury Lane met for the most part with failure.

The pamphlet that followed, *Chit-Chat,* appeared only three times, on March 3 (?), 10, 16, and the first of these is lost. Though the format is similar, the topic is different, involving a defense of Steele himself rather than the reformation of Drury Lane. Steele had followed an independent course in Parliament, and on one explosive issue he had publicly disagreed with the Whig leaders. The Jacobite lords who had assisted the invasion of British soil by the Pretender had been sentenced to death; to the chagrin of Whig leaders in Parliament Steele took issue publicly with this harsh decision, calling instead for mercy and magnanimity. Steele had always been recognized as a staunch Whig, but now because of his independent course he was accused of secret leanings to Jacobitism, of receiving bribes, and of leaving the Whigs. All of these accusations were false, but he felt the need to defend himself in print. The persona for *Chit-Chat* is Humphrey Philroye, a Hanoverian Whig who is interested in public affairs and describes them to a lady in the country. Philroye is especially interested in the career of Richard Steele, although he rejects Steele's plea for mercy toward the condemned lords. Nevertheless, Humphrey praises Steele for his independent thinking: "Sir Richard Steele has ever acted an uniform, sometimes a dangerous Part; and I am sure that those Persons are very servile, and know little of the Blessings of the Freedom of a Subject, or a Man, who tack themselves necessarily to Vote with their Leaders; and can't, with Candour and Good-nature, be allow'd to dissent sometimes in Opinion with their best Friends" (*Chit-Chat,* No. 3).

Unfortunately, Steele's outspokenness caused him other difficulties. His disagreement in print with Addison over political issues helped their remarkable friendship to disintegrate, and Addison's death in 1719 while unreconciled to Steele must have left its mark.[14] No less disquieting was the instability of Steele's major source of income, the governorship of Drury Lane. He insisted again on his independence, this time from the control of the Lord Chamberlain, the young Duke of Newcastle, and as a result Newcastle threatened to take legal action against Steele's patent and remove both control of Drury Lane and the profits

from him. The unpleasant legal struggle between Newcastle and
Steele is shared with the reading public in *The Theatre,* which
was Steele's attempt at self-defense. He had little chance to defeat
Newcastle, and his angry disputation in print did nothing to
resolve the issue.

"*The Theatre,* which appeared in half-sheet issues twice weekly
from 2 January 1720 to 5 April 1720, proved to be Steele's final
periodical, and indeed his final extended literary production."[15]
The persona Steele chose for *The Theatre* is Sir John Edgar, the
earlier name for Sir John Bevil of *The Conscious Lovers.* The characters from that play also appear in *The Theatre;* it is likely therefore that the play was written but not in its final draft, and that
Steele chose to make use of it for his immediate needs.[16] The
excellent possibilities of adapting his play to a serial publication
elude him, however, and instead *The Theatre* becomes Steele's
personal cry of anguish against the injustices he feels he has
endured.[17] In a letter signed by Steele appears a proud yet pathetic
insistence on his independence: "I would not hurt any Man now
in India, for the Favour of the greatest Man in *England,* or give
up a Door-keeper of the Play-house to make myself so" (no. 8).
By the time of its conclusion with its twenty-eighth number on
April 5, Steele's spirit had been severely tried, perhaps irrecov-
erably broken; his wife Prue had died in 1718, Addison had died
in 1719, and he had lost his Patent in 1720, and he was now
struggling simply to support his children and survive. *The Theatre*
had not helped his public image; in fact, even he realized that
the whining tone must have offended readers. He asks pardon
of his readers with this apology: "I desire any Man, who judges
of it, to consider it as it is, not the Product of a Mind at Ease,
but written by a Man neither out of Pain in Body or Mind; but
forced to suspend the Anguish of both, with the Addition of
powerful Men soliciting my Ruin, shy Looks from my Acquaintance, surly Behavior from my Domesticks, with all the Train of
private and publick Calamity, and that for no other Reason but
pursuing what he thought just, and then let him say to himself,
whether he could carry his Gaiety much further than I have" (no.
28).

The final paragraph of his final periodical begins with this unsettlingly pathetic resolution: "I shall not whine longer about the Hardships I have suffer'd." This is indeed a changed man from the Steele who wrote the *Tatler,* the *Spectator,* and four comedies. It is Steele defeated by political ingratitude, by financial mismanagement, and by poor health. He did experience a last blaze of glory with the appearance of *The Conscious Lovers* in 1722, but this play had been in the works years earlier, perhaps as early as 1711 and 1712. Shortly thereafter—in poor health— Steele retired in 1724 to his wife's estate in Wales where he remained until his death in 1729.

Notes and References

Chapter One

1. Calhoun Winton, *Captain Steele* (Baltimore: The Johns Hopkins Press, 1964), pp. 1–60. Professor Winton's book is a well-documented and well-written biography essential for an understanding of Steele and his writings.

2. Winton, *Captain Steele,* pp. 20–26.

3. Richard Steele, *The Theatre,* no. 11, ed. John Loftis (Oxford: Clarendon Press, 1962), p. 49.

4. Richard Steele, *The Christian Hero,* ed. Rae Blanchard (London: Humphrey Milford, 1932), pp. x, xi. Hereafter page references cited in the text.

5. Rae Blanchard, "Richard Steele and the Status of Women," *Studies in Philology* 26 (1929): 325–55.

6. Steele's defense of women was a significant force in improving the status of women and changing the attitudes of men in England. In her edition of *The Christian Hero* Professor Rae Blanchard lists numerous references by Steele to the contemporary manifestation of feminism. His concern with women is conspicuous in much of his later work, both his periodicals and his plays.

7. Staring B. Wells, ed. *A Comparison Between the Two Stages—A Late Restoration Book of the Theatre* (Princeton: Princeton University Press, 1942), p. 87. The critic insinuates that the title page was merely canceled to make it look as though there had been a reprinting: "It was but once printed, nor is all that Impression sold; 'tis a Trick of the Bookseller's to get it off."

8. Richard Steele, *Mr. Steele's Apology for Himself and his Writings,* in *Tracts and Pamphlets of Richard Steele,* ed. Rae Blanchard (Baltimore: The Johns Hopkins Press, 1944), p. 339.

9. C. Lennart Carlson, "Samuel Keimer," *Pennsylvania Magazine of History and Biography* 41 (1937): 359.

10. Ibid., p. 375.

11. Friedrich Christoph Schlosser, *History of the Eighteenth Century* (London: Chapman and Hall, 1843), 1:102.

12. William Makepeace Thackeray, "The English Humourists of the Eighteenth Century," *Works* (New York: Charles Scribner's Sons, 1904), pp. 243–44.

13. Donald G. Mitchell, *English Lands, Letters and Kings, from Elizabeth to Anne* (New York: Charles Scribner's Sons, 1890), p. 281.

14. Austin Dobson, *Richard Steele* (London: Longmans, Green, 1888), p. 22.

15. Richard Steele, *The Christian Hero,* ed. Rae Blanchard (London, 1932), pp. ix–xxxii, 3–101.

16. Ibid., p. xii.

Credit should be given to Harold Routh's essay on Steele in the *Cambridge History of English Literature.* Routh lets biographical information affect his judgment at times, but he nevertheless presents a reasonably accurate account of *CH*.

In the *Times Literary Supplement* (London) for Thursday, October 13, 1932, an anonymous reviewer evaluates Professor Blanchard's edition of *CH,* unfortunately referring to her as a male. Unfortunately too, the reviewer is influenced by the worst of the nineteenth-century critics: "Steele had so much in him of natural, middle-class humanity that the proud and lonely self-reliance of Stoicism meant as little to him as the classics in general meant to the new aspirants after culture and refinement."

Chapter Two

1. *Mr. Steele's Apology for Himself and His Writings,* The *Tracts and Pamphlets of Richard Steele,* ed. Rae Blanchard (Baltimore: The Johns Hopkins Press, 1944; rpt. 1967), p. 339. Hereafter cited in text as *Ap* followed by page number.

2. Shirley Strum Kenny, ed., *The Plays of Richard Steele* (Oxford: Clarendon Press, 1971), p. 6. Hereafter page references cited in text.

3. Elvena M. Green, "Three Aspects of Richard Steele's Theory of Comedy," *Educational Theatre Journal* 20 (1968):141.

4. Robert A. Aubin, "Behind Steele's Satire on Undertakers," *PMLA* 64 (1949):1021. Aubin points to causes and subsequent effects of this relatively rapid social change: "In short, theology, sentimental concern for the material needs of the dead, and the social pretensions of the rising middle class worked together between 1680 and 1700 to create a wide demand for embalmment, coffin burial, funeral show, and made-to-order heraldry,—the 'most sollid' funeral. The way was open for the popular purveyor of these goods and services."

5. Winton, *Captain Steele,* p. 63.

6. "He knows h' has num'rous Friends, nay knows they'll show it, / And for the Fellow-Soldier save the Poet."

7. Shirley Strum Kenny, "Steele and the Pattern of Genteel Comedy," *Modern Philology* 70 (1972):23.

8. Not included among these comic scenes is Sharlot's leaping out of the coffin to the obvious amazement of all present, which fails to be comic.

9. Shirley Kenny describes Trim as "an eighteenth-century Walter Mitty," in "Genteel Comedy," p. 26.

10. Winton, *Captain Steele,* p. 62.

11. Susan Staves, "Liars and Lying in Alarcón, Corneille, and Steele," *Revue de Littérature Comparée* 46 (1972):514–27. "Steele's play is an adaptation of one of Pierre Corneille's best comedies, *Le Menteur,* first performed in Paris in 1643. In its turn *Le Menteur* was an adaptation of Ruiz de Alarcón's *La verdad sospechosa* (publ. 1621), perhaps one of the best comedies of the Golden Age" (515).

12. See V, iii, where Old Bookwit says of his son, "I doubt not but his future Carriage wou'd deserve her."

13. John F. Tatton, "Richard Steele and Terence" (Ph.D. diss., University of Texas, 1970), p. 105. Tatton discusses "the school tradition of Terence" which Steele used "in reforming the morals of his age" (106).

14. Rae Blanchard, "Richard Steele as a Moralist and Social Reformer" (Ph.D. diss., University of Chicago, 1927), p. 82. "In general the points which he brings out are that there must be mutual respect and sympathy; that the father should govern by love, not force; and that affection between them should be emotional."

15. For differing opinions on sentimental comedy in *The Tender Husband,* see Ernest Bernbaum, *The Drama of Sensibility* (Gloucester, Mass.: Peter Smith, 1958), p. 101n, and Arthur Sherbo, *English Sentimental Drama* (East Lansing: Michigan State University Press, 1957), pp. 105–106.

16. Perhaps the best term for *The Tender Husband* is Humane Comedy, characterized generally by good nature but with characters who are mixtures of good and bad. The term comes from Shirley Strum Kenny and Calhoun Winton, who presented a paper on "New Directions in English Drama" at the East Central meeting of the American Society for Eighteenth Century Studies, Duquesne University, October 1978. In describing Humane Comedy, they say: "There is good humor about these plays; one finds reduced expectations for the human spirit, per-

haps, but also greater tolerance for its follies—cynicism is supplanted by cheerful acceptance of human limitation." This is precisely the attitude apparent in *The Tender Husband.*

17. Richard Steele, *The Tender Husband,* ed. Calhoun Winton (Lincoln: University of Nebraska Press, 1967), p. xii. Hereafter cited in text as *TH,* followed by page number.

18. John Loftis, *Comedy and Society from Congreve to Fielding* (Stanford: Stanford University Press, 1959), p. 64.

19. Winton, ed., *The Tender Husband,* p. xviii, and Kenny, "Steele and the Pattern of Genteel Comedy," *Modern Philology* 70 (1972):30. Winton says that Clerimont Senior is "a thoroughgoing brute," whereas Kenny calls him "a patient man as well as a tender husband."

20. Loftis, *Comedy and Society,* p. 64.

21. For insight into heroic romances and heroic drama, see Leslie H. Martin, "Conventions of the French Romances in the Drama of John Dryden" (Ph.D. diss., Stanford University, 1967).

22. Self-interest and clever practicality lead Biddy and Humphry through a parody of the proviso scene best known from Congreve's *The Way of the World.* In act 3, scene 2, Biddy and Humphry list, in dialogue form, their reasons for *not* marrying each other. As a result of their clear understanding, which is of course the purpose of a proviso scene, Biddy and Humphry are able to conspire together in order to achieve their separate goals.

23. Blanchard, "Social Reformer," p. 83.

24. Loftis, *Comedy and Society,* p. 75.

25. John Harrington Smith, "Tony Lumpkin and the Country Booby Type in Antecedent English Comedy," *PMLA* 58 (1943):1038–49. Humphry is "an original creation of high merit, and one from which not only Goldsmith, but other subsequent writers, derived numerous hints" (1040).

26. Shirley Strum Kenny, "Two Scenes by Addison in Steele's *Tender Husband,*" *Studies in Bibliography* 19 (1966):217–26.

Chapter Three

1. See Tatton, "Richard Steele and Terence," (Ph.D. diss., University of Texas, 1970) and Bernbaum, *The Drama of Sensibility,* pp. 11–26. Tatton suggests that "Steele's interpretation of the Terention sententia . . . had become widely recognized as both a symbol and precedent for the popular ethos of Christian benevolence" (3).

2. John Dennis, "Remarks on a Play, Call'd, *The Conscious Lovers,* Comedy," *The Critical Works of John Dennis,* ed. Edward Niles Hooker (Baltimore: The Johns Hopkins Press, 1943), 2:251–74.

3. Shirley Strum Kenny, Introduction to *The Conscious Lovers* (Lincoln: University of Nebraska Press, 1968), p. xiv.

4. Richard Steele, *The Theatre,* ed. John Loftis (Oxford: Clarendon Press, 1962), p. 83.

5. See John Harrington Smith, *The Gay Couple in Restoration Comedy* (Cambridge: Harvard University Press, 1948), pp. 45–81; 193–232.

6. John Loftis, *Steele at Drury Lane* (Berkeley: University of California Press, 1952), p. 202. Loftis says that Bevil, Jr., "is, and was recognized to be by Steele's contemporaries, an embodiment of precisely the contrary moral qualities of those exhibited by the Restoration gallants, who people the comedies of Etherege, Dryden, Wycherley, and Congreve; he owes his existence to Steele's conviction . . . [that] the display of debauched characters on the stage was damaging to the morals of the spectators."

7. Bevil, Jr., is called an unfashionable lover by Indiana; yet he is beginning a new fashion which will expel those like Tom who consider themselves the very quintessence of fashion, "the Representative of all better fed than taught."

8. Bevil, Jr., exclaims, "Let him be Provident, but let me be Happy"; the ideal of the play, however, is in a balance between the sentiments of father and son.

9. Isabella says: "I once had almost as much love for a Man, who poorly left me, to marry an Estate" (332).

10. Loftis, *Comedy and Society,* p. 83.

11. Ibid., p. 84. Loftis prints a memorandum by Steele indicating the purpose of his characterization. The dialogue appears in act 4, scene 2.

12. For a further discussion, see Rae Blanchard, "Richard Steele and the Status of Women," *Studies in Philology* 26 (1929):325–55. "Considering the social customs of his age, Steele's persistent efforts to bring about one standard of sex morality and matrimonial fidelity were remarkable" (349).

13. Smith, *The Gay Couple,* p. 209.

14. See act 2, scene 1, pp. 15–17. "And you know I have ever told you, you might make use of my secret Resolution never to marry her, for your own service, as you please."

15. At the end of act 3, Cimberton, blithely unaware of the fraud perpetrated on him, says: "The Vulgar would have no respect for Truth

and Knowledge, if they were exposed to naked View. Truth is too simple, of all Art bereav'd: Since the World will—why let it be deceived."

16. Grimgribber became a term denoting gibberish.

17. In act 2, scene 1, Bevil, Jr. says: "It would be an immoral thing to mock him, were it not that this Impertinence is the occasion of its breaking out to that degree."

18. Bernbaum, *The Drama of Sensibility,* p. 136.

Chapter Four

1. *The Tatler,* ed. G. A. Aitken (London: Duckworth and Co., 1898), 1:8. All references in the text are to this edition. Numbers in parentheses refer to numbers of the *Tatler,* not pages. This chapter focuses on the essays by Steele; Professor Otten's Twayne study, *Joseph Addison,* examines those essays by Addison.

2. Under the pen of Bickerstaff, Steele writes: "The state of conversation and business in this town having been long perplexed with pretenders in both kinds, in order to open men's eyes against such abuses, it appeared no unprofitable undertaking to publish a paper which should observe upon the manners of the pleasurable, as well as the busy part of mankind" (1:7). This would sound haughty and overbearing from Richard Steele, whereas it is acceptable from the grandfatherly Bickerstaff.

3. Richmond P. Bond, *The Tatler—The Making of a Literary Journal* (Cambridge: Harvard University Press, 1971), pp. 67, 68. Bond's book offers essential research on Steele, Bickerstaff, and the *Tatler.*

4. Bickerstaff became very specific about some of his personal experience, even to the extreme of complaining about a toothache.

5. See Bond, *The Tatler,* p. 242N37.

6. See the description of Bickerstaff's genealogy, with a delightfully subtle attack on pride of birth, in No. 75.

7. Note, for example, the mention of his departed friend John Partridge in No. 96, and the announcement that "a commission of interment has been awarded against Dr. John Partridge" in No. 99. Fortunately, Steele did not overdo what might have become an old joke.

8. In *Tatler* 71 Bickerstaff places his dilemma in the extreme: "Giving disturbance, though not intended, to men of virtuous characters, has so sincerely troubled me, that I will break from this satirical vein . . . and touch on nothing but panegyric."

9. See Louis T. Milic, "Tone in Steele's *'Tatler,'* " *Newsletters to Newspapers: Eighteenth-Century Journalism,* ed. D. H. Bond and W. R. McLeod (Morgantown: West Virginia University, 1977), pp. 33–45; and Ruth Allen Cameron, "The Prose Style of Addison and Steele in the Periodical Essay" (Ph.D. diss., Boston University, 1972).

10. See the allegory on Conscience and Honor in *Tatler* 48. For further discussion of Steele's attitude toward the double standard, see Blanchard, "Status of Women," and her "Richard Steele as a Moralist and Social Reformer" (Ph.D. diss., University of Chicago, 1927).

11. See *Tatler* 86, 164, 203, 207, 258. Note Steele's moral theory from *The Christian Hero* with a slightly different emphasis: "Nothing is laudable but what is guided by reason" (180).

12. "The possession of four thousand pounds gave my young gentleman a new train of thoughts: he began to reflect upon his birth, the great expectations he was born to, and the unsuitable ways he had long pursued. Instead of that unthinking creature he was before, he is now provident, generous, and discreet. The father and son have an exact and regular correspondence, with mutual and unreserved confidence in each other" (60).

13. The curiously harsh satire on Mary Astell and the "platonic ladies" reveals how strongly Steele reacted against women who sought independence from men.

14. One of Bickerstaff 's most eloquent papers on marriage is *Tatler* 150, wherein he discourages couples from arguing about trivial differences, all the while praising the "excellent institution" of marriage.

15. See *The Tatler,* ed. Aitken, 3:394n, 395n. For satiric reference to absolutism in Rome, see the letters from Pasquin in *Tatler* 187.

16. Bond, *The Tatler,* p. 110. "Bickerstaff gave [Milton] more attention than any other English writer except Shakespeare, and in so doing he made no small contribution to literary criticism in the early periodical press."

17. Ibid., p. 111. "In the *Tatler* it received a warm, sensible, unpretentious judgement."

In *Tatler* 237 Bickerstaff uses *Paradise Lost* for a discussion of the disguises of mankind and the power of Ithuriel's spear.

18. Signior Nicolini, who received the praise, was acting in an opera, a form of entertainment to which Steele was usually opposed. "On Saturday night last the opera of 'Pyrrhus and Demetrius' was performed with great applause. This intelligence is not very acceptable to us friends of the theatre; for the stage being an entertainment of the reason and all our faculties, this way of being pleased with the suspense of them

for three hours together, and being given up to the shallow satisfaction of the eyes and ears only, seems to arise rather from the degeneracy of our understanding, than an improvement of our diversions" (4).

19. "Among the modern, indeed there has arisen a chimerical method of disposing the fortune of the persons represented, according to what they call poetical justice; and letting none be unhappy, but those who deserve it" (82).

20. Conversely, the savage diversions of the town, such as bear-baiting and cockfighting, and the drunken ignorance of nature found in the country receive Bickerstaff's strong criticism. Part of the purpose of the *Tatler* is to reclaim both the ignorant and the savage, so that they may be civil, virtuous, and if possible benevolent.

21. One would like to know if T. S. talked to his flowers.

Chapter Five

1. Donald F. Bond, ed., Introduction to *The Spectator* (Oxford: Clarendon Press, 1965), pp. xiii—cix. Bond's introduction to his five-volume edition is an excellent scholarly study of the *Spectator,* indeed the best collection of information available. Numbers in parentheses refer to numbers of the *Spectator,* not pages.

2. Ibid., p. lvi.

3. Ibid., p. lix. "About two out of every three papers with Steele's signature letters are made up on contributed matter, sometimes with a sentence or two by way of introduction, at other times with no editorial comment whatever. Hence, while it is true to say that the two men shared equal responsibility for the 555 numbers, Addison's contribution in the form of original essays looms much larger."

4. See John Gay, *The Present State of Wit* (London, 1711; rpt. New York: Garland Press, 1970), pp. 13—14. " 'Tis incredible to conceive the Effect his Writings have had on the Town."

5. See *Spectator* 2 for the Club.

6. See *Spectator* 350, 352.

7. Mr. Spectator discusses the value of being a spectator in 454 and encourages his readers to share his interest and positive attitude toward other people: "I thought it of great Use, if they could learn with me to keep their Minds open to Gratification, and ready to receive it from any thing it meets with. This one Circumstance will make every Face you see give you the Satisfaction you now take in beholding that of a Friend; will make every Object a pleasing one; will make all

the Good which arrives to any Man, an Encrease of Happiness to your self."

8. Bond, *The Spectator,* p. lxv. This chapter will examine Steele's contribution to the *Spectator.* For Addison's part in these essays, one should see Professor Robert Otten's book on Joseph Addison in this series. For additional information see the following:

Donald F. Bond, "The First Printing of the *Spectator,*" *Modern Philology* 47 (1950):164–77.

Melvin R. Watson, "The *Spectator* Tradition and the Development of the Familiar Essay," *English Literary History* 13 (1946):189–215.

John Loftis, "The Blenheim Papers and Steele's Journalism, 1715–18," *PMLA* 64 (1951):197–210.

Donald F. Bond, "Pope's Contributions to the *Spectator,*" *Modern Language Quarterly* 5 (1944):69–78.

Donald F. Bond, "The Text of the *Spectator,*" *Studies in Bibliography* 5 (1953):109–28.

9. See *Spectator* 48.

10. In *Spectator* 312 Mr. Spectator advocates moderation as a valuable approach to the joys and the sufferings of life: "Moderation . . . is peculiar to generous Minds."

11. See *Spectator* 448, 218, 212, 294, 443, 346, 428, 274, 456.

12. Steele may have written this letter to himself; whether it came from a correspondent or from Steele is not relevant.

13. See *Spectator* 182, 190, 260, 318, 462.

14. See Kenny, Introduction to *Plays.*

15. Steele satirizes jealousy between husband and wife as one of the banes of marriage (178, 194), and he considers marriage forced by parents or relatives an intolerable injustice leading to a lifetime of hatred (308, 455).

16. Steele describes his ideal: "He that sincerely loves his Wife and Family, and studies to improve that Affection in himself, conceives Pleasure from the most indifferent things; while the married Man who has not bid adieu to the Fashions and false Gallantries of the Town, is perplexed with every thing around him" (479).

17. See Donald Kay, *Short Fiction in "The Spectator"* (University: University of Alabama Press, 1975). "Steele wrote most of the stories of a domestic nature," says Kay (123).

18. The conclusion of *Spectator* 342 is a shock to anyone who considers Steele a feminist. Women, he says, "will in no part of their Lives want Opportunities of being shining Ornaments to their Fathers, Husbands, Brothers or Children."

19. See *Spectator* 187, 272, 320, 348, 427, 392, 334, 515.

20. Steele discussed the ethical problem of prostitution in *Spectators* 266 and 274.

21. See also *Spectator* 326, 328, 486.

22. For various examples, see *Spectator* 172, 178, 202, 84, 76, 97, 480, 230.

23. See *Spectator* 259, 280, 386, 422, 424, 430, 520.

24. See *Spectator* 340, 139, 206, 152.

25. See *Spectator* 172.

Chapter Six

1. Virgil, *The Aeneid*, ed. Rolfe Humphries (New York: Scribner's, 1951).

2. Joseph Addison and Richard Steele, *Selected Essays from "The Tatler," "The Spectator," and "The Guardian,"* ed. Daniel McDonald (New York: Bobbs-Merrill Co., 1973), p. 583. McDonald's Introduction is eminently readable and worthwhile.

3. *The Guardian* (London: J. Tonson, 1713), in *English Literary Periodicals of the 17th, 18th, and 19th Centuries*, No. E182, Reel 949, *Guardian* No. 6.

4. Winton, *Captain Steele*, p. 163.

5. One is indeed perplexed with Steele's potentially outrageous pun in *Guardian* No. 6, where Nestor writes: "It is a Fault in all Ministries that they encourage no kind of Horses but those which are swift." Steele, of course, felt that Swift was instrumental in the *Examiner*, the Tory ministry's publication.

The modern edition of *The Englishman* is once again the work of Rae Blanchard: Richard Steele, *The Englishman*, ed. Rae Blanchard (Oxford: Clarendon Press, 1955), pp. vii–xxii, 1–497.

See also Calhoun Winton's chapter on *The Englishman* in *Captain Steele*.

6. Richard Steele, *The Lover*, in *Steele's Periodical Journalism 1714–16*, ed. Rae Blanchard (Oxford: Clarendon Press, 1959), p. 11.

7. Ibid., (No. 2), p. 10.

8. *The Christian Hero*, pp. 77–78. Rae Blanchard says in her introduction that in Steele's analysis of human psychology "the passions are the Springs of Human Action, whose important function it is to motivate conduct. . . . Every action has its origin in a passion" (xiv).

9. *The Lover*, pp. 30–31. The following statement corroborates Steele's theory of the passions and reason expressed in *The Christian*

Hero, wherein he argues that reason, strengthened by religion, may guide, direct, and reform a passion so that the passion itself becomes a moving force to virtue and benevolence:

In the Calculation of a Man's Happiness in Life, there is no one Circumstance which ought more carefully to be considered, than the Object of one's Love. . . . It is the utmost Madness to let your Affection fix where you cannot expect the Approbation of your Reason. If a Man does not take this Precaution, his Days will pass away with frivolous Pleasures and solid Vexations.

10. Richard Steele, *The Reader,* in *Steele's Periodical Journalism 1714–16,* ed. Rae Blanchard (Oxford: Clarendon Press, 1959), p. 143. Steele's persona—the reader who writes the paper—defines himself in terms of his displeasure with periodicals imposing upon innocent readers their misleading and biased information:

You must know I have a long Time frequented Coffeehouses and read Papers, and spent my Money upon Coffee for the Advantage of Reading the Papers; tho' the Coffee and the Papers also are meer Dryers and do but hinder my natural Capacity by a forced Liveliness as to the Coffee, and a false Gravity as to the Papers; for as to the former, I have afterwards found my self dispirited thereby, as to the latter mis-led rather than enlightened.

11. See Blanchard, ed., *The Reader,* pp. 291–92.
12. See Blanchard, Introduction to *Town-Talk,* pp. xxi–xxiii.
13. John Loftis, *Steele at Drury Lane* (Berkeley: University of California Press, 1952), p. 244.
14. Winton, *Sir Richard Steele,* pp. 160–63.
15. Richard Steele, *The Theatre,* ed. John Loftis (Oxford: Clarendon Press, 1962), p. ix.
16. The dueling scene of *The Conscious Lovers* is in the fourth act, but in the *Theatre* no. 19 he refers to it as in the third act. See pp. 83, 136.
17. For excellent, detailed discussions of Steele's plight in the later days of his career, see Calhoun Winton's biography *Sir Richard Steele* and John Loftis's analysis of the issues surrounding the Drury Lane Patent in *Steele at Drury Lane.* Loftis's edition of *The Theatre* offers a useful introduction as well.

Selected Bibliography

PRIMARY SOURCES

The Christian Hero. Edited by Rae Blanchard. London: Humphrey Milford, 1932.

The Conscious Lovers. Edited by Shirley Strum Kenny. Regents Restoration Drama Series. Lincoln: University of Nebraska, 1968.

The Correspondence of Richard Steele. Edited by Rae Blanchard. Oxford: Humphrey Milford, 1941.

The Englishman. Edited by Rae Blanchard. Oxford: Clarendon Press, 1955.

The Guardian. In *English Literary Periodicals of the 17th, 18th, and 19th Centuries,* No. E182, Reel 949. London: J. Tonson, 1713.

The Occasional Verse of Richard Steele. Edited by Rae Blanchard. Oxford: Clarendon Press, 1952.

The Plays of Richard Steele. Edited by Shirley Strum Kenny. Oxford: Clarendon Press, 1971. See *PQ* 51, no. 3 (July, 1972):770 for review by Curt A. Zimansky.

Richard Steele's Periodical Journalism, 1714–16. Edited by Rae Blanchard. Oxford: Clarendon Press, 1959. *The Lover, The Reader, Town-Talk in a Letter to a Lady in the Country, Chit-Chat in a Letter to a Lady in the Country.*

The Spectator. Edited by Donald F. Bond. 5 vols. Oxford: Clarendon Press, 1965.

The Tatler. Edited by George A. Aitken. 4 vols. London: Duckworth and Co., 1898–99.

The Tender Husband. Edited by Calhoun Winton. Regents Restoration Drama Series. Lincoln: University of Nebraska Press, 1967.

The Theatre. Edited by John Loftis. Oxford: Clarendon Press, 1962.

Tracts and Pamphlets by Richard Steele. Edited by Rae Blanchard. Baltimore: The Johns Hopkins Press, 1944; rpt. New York: Octagon Books, 1967.

SECONDARY SOURCES

1. Books

Aitken, George A. *The Life of Richard Steele.* 2 vols, 1889; rpt. New York: Greenwood Press, 1968. The best biography of Richard Steele before Calhoun Winton's two volumes in 1964 and 1970.

Bloom, Edward A., and Bloom, Lillian D. *Addison and Steele The Critical Heritage.* London: Routledge and Kegan Paul, 1980. Highlights the separate identities of the two men and documents their reputations by concentrating largely upon eighteenth-century criticism.

Bond, Richard P. *New Letters to the "Tatler" and "Spectator."* Austin: University of Texas Press, 1959. The editor brings together ninety-six heretofore unpublished letters to the *Tatler* and the *Spectator.*

————. *The Pirate and the Tatler.* London: The Bibliography Society, 1965; rpt. from *The Library,* 5th ser., 18 (1963):257–274. Discusses the problem of pirate printers in the early 18th Century, specifically regarding the *Tatler.*

————. *Studies in the Early English Periodical.* Chapel Hill: University of North Carolina Press, 1957. An essential study of the periodical.

————. *The Tatler: The Making of a Literary Journal.* Cambridge: Harvard University Press, 1971. The essential study of *The Tatler.*

Evans, James E., and Wall, John F., Jr. *A Guide to Prose Fiction in The Tatler and The Spectator.* New York: Garland Publishing, 1977. An introduction worth examining together with a useful reference collection.

Gay, John. *The Present State of Wit* (London: 1711), pp. 5–23. Praises both *The Tatler* and *The Spectator* very highly.

Goldgar, Bertrand A. *The Curse of Party.* Lincoln: The University of Nebraska Press, 1961. Required reading for an understanding of the intense animosity between Swift and Steele.

Kay, Donald. *Short Fiction in the Spectator.* University: University of Alabama Press, 1975. A sound study of the approximately 100 pieces of fiction in the *Spectator* by Addison and Steele.

Loftis, John. *Comedy and Society from Congreve to Fielding.* Stanford: Stanford University Press, 1959. The second book of three on the political theme in drama.

————. *The Politics of Drama in Augustan England.* Oxford: Clarendon Press, 1963. The final book of three on the political theme in drama.

————. *Steele at Drury Lane.* Berkeley and Los Angeles: University of California Press, 1952. The standard scholarly work for this period. See reviews in *Philological Quarterly* 32:294; *Modern Language Notes* 68:276–77; *Journal of English and Germanic Philology* 51:601–4; and *Modern Philology* 50:64–67.

Smith, John Harrington. *The Gay Couple in Restoration Comedy.* Cambridge: Harvard University Press, 1948. Important discussion of the gay and serious couple.

Winton, Calhoun. *Captain Steele—The Early Career of Richard Steele.* Baltimore: Johns Hopkins Press, 1964. The first volume of Winton's two-volume biography of Steele.

————. *Sir Richard Steele, M.P.* Baltimore: Johns Hopkins Press, 1970. The second volume of the biography. Both volumes are indispensable.

2. Articles

Achurch, Robert Waller. "Richard Steele Gazeteer and Bickerstaff." In *Studies in the Early English Periodical,* edited by Richmond P. Bond, pp. 49–72. Chapel Hill: University of North Carolina Press, 1957. Examines the relationship between the *Gazette* and the *Tatler.*

Allen, Robert J. "Contemporary Allusions in *The Tatler.*" *Modern Language Notes* 40 (1940):292–94. Steele used contemporary personalities and incidents as material for the *Tatler.* Allen refers to letters written by the daughter and the sister of Robert Harley.

————. "Steele and the Molesworth Family." *Review of English Studies* 12 (1936):449–54. The identity of the characters described in *Tatler* 189.

————. "William Oldisworth: 'the Author of *The Examiner.*' " *Philological Quarterly* 26 (1947):173. Jonathan Swift preceded Oldisworth as editor of a party journal.

Appleton, William W. "The Double Gallant in Eighteenth Century Comedy." In *English Writers of the Eighteenth Century,* edited by John H. Middendorf, pp. 145–57. New York: Columbia University Press, 1971. Read in conjunction with Smith's *The Gay Couple.*

Aubin, Robert A. "Behind Steele's Satire on Undertakers." *PMLA* 44 (1949):1008–26. Aubin's chief purpose is to describe the evolution of undertaking and Steele's use of it as an object of satire in *The Funeral.*

Averill, James H. "The Death of Stephen Clay and Richard Steele's *Spectators* of August 1711." *Review of English Studies,* n.s. 28 (1977):305–10. Describes the actual experience behind *The Spectator* in August, 1711, namely the death of Steele's lawyer and friend, Stephen Clay.

Baine, Rodney M. "The Publication of Steele's *Conscious Lovers.*" *Studies in Bibliography* 2 (1949–50):170–73. Discusses the publication rights and payment for *The Conscious Lovers.*

Betz, Sigmond A. E. "The Operatic Criticism of the *Tatler* and *Spectator.*" *Musical Quarterly* 31 (1945):318–30. A general attack on Steele, Addison, and Dennis concerning their dislike of Italian opera.

Blanchard, Rae. "Additions to *The Correspondence of Richard Steele.*" *Review of English Studies* 18 (1942):466–70. Additional letters.

————. "Another Steele Letter." *Review of English Studies* 23 (1947):147–52. Commentary on mutual affairs of Addison and Steele.

————. "*The Christian Hero,* by Richard Steele: a bibliography." *Library,* 4th series (1929), pp. 61–72. This information derives from Blanchard's preparation of her edition of *The Christian Hero.*

————. "A Prologue and Epilogue for Nicholas Rowe's *Tamerlane* by Richard Steele." *PMLA* 47 (1932):772–76. Steele's contribution to Rowe.

————. "Richard Steele and the Secretary of the SPCK." In *Restoration and Eighteenth-Century Literature,* edited by Carroll Camden, pp. 287–96. Chicago: University of Chicago Press, 1963. Recently available letters of Henry Newman show the friendly relations between the two men and shed occasional light on some of Steele's essays.

————. "Richard Steele and the Status of Women." *Studies in Philology* 26 (1929):325–55. Examines Steele's views about women as expressed in his essays.

————. "Richard Steele and William Lord Cowper: New Letters." *PMLA* 80 (1965):303–06. Seven hitherto unpublished letters written by Steele to Lord Cowper between 1710/11 and 1720.

————. "Richard Steele's Maryland Story." *American Quarterly* 10 (1958):78–82. The story of the American Negro in *The Lover* (No. 36, May 18, 1714) is an early specimen of primitivism.

————. "Richard Steele's West Indian Plantation." *Modern Philology* 39 (1942):281–85. Information concerning Steele's financial transactions.

————. "Some Unpublished Letters of Richard Steele to the Duke of Newcastle." *Modern Language Notes* 48 (1933):232–46. The Duke of Newcastle posed the threat to Steele's control of and earnings from the Patent at Drury Lane.

————. "The Songs in Steele's Plays." In *Pope and His Contemporaries: Essays Presented to George Sherburn,* edited by James L. Clifford and Louis A. Landa, pp. 185–200. Oxford: Clarendon Press, 1949. Songs serve to highlight character and situation.

————. "Steele and Chesterfield." *Review of English Studies* 20 (1944):63–67. Discusses a letter to Steele from the *third* Earl of Chesterfield.

————. "Steele, Charles King, and the Dunkirk Pamphlets." *Huntington Library Quarterly* 14 (1951):423–29. Discussion of very rare pamphlet.

————. "Steeleiana: an eighteenth-century account book." *Studies in Philology* 39 (1942):502–09. Adds information about Hannah Maria Keck, friend of Lady Steele.

————. "Steele's *Christian Hero* and the *errata* in the *Tatler*." *Review of English Studies* 6 (1930):183–85. Argues that Steele as well as Addison provided stylistic revision for the *Tatler*.

————. "Was Richard Steele a Freemason?" *PMLA* 63 (1948):903–17. Suggests that Steele indeed was a Freemason.

Bloom, Edward A. and Bloom, Lillian D. "Steele in 1719: Additions to the Canon." *Huntington Library Quarterly* 31 (1968):123–51. Provides letters against the Peerage Bill of 1719.

————. "Steele and His Answerers: May 1709–February 1714." 167–97. White, Robert B., Jr., ed. *The Dress of Words: Essays on Restoration and Eighteenth Century Literature in Honor of Richmond P. Bond.* (University of Kansas Pubs., Lib. Ser. 42) Lawrence: Univ. of Kansas Libs., 1978. Detailed account of the first of Steele's paper wars with the Tories. Analyzes Mrs. Manley's attack on Steele, then the attacks of the various papers and concludes that in this first paper war Steele proved himself as a rhetorician.

Bond, Donald F. "Armand de la Chapelle and The First French Version of the Tatler." In *Restoration and Eighteenth-Century Literature,* edited by Carroll Camden, pp. 161–84. Chicago: University of Chicago Press, 1963.

————. "The First Printing of the *Spectator*." *Modern Philology* 47 (1950):164–77. The original 555 numbers of the *Spectator* were printed in two shops—those of Samuel Buckley and, probably, Jacob Tonson.

Bond, Richmond P. "Isaac Bickerstaff, Esq." In *Restoration and Eighteenth-Century Literature,* edited by Carroll Camden, pp. 103–24. Chicago: University of Chicago Press, 1963. Describes Swift's and Steele's Bickerstaff.

————. "John Partridge and the Company of Stationers." *Studies in Bibliography* 16 (1963):75–79. Discusses a plan to introduce an almanac under Bickerstaff's name.

————. "A Letter to Steele on *The Spectator*." *Modern Language Quarterly* 18 (1957):303–04. From Joseph Collet, employee of East India Company.

————. "Mr. Bickerstaff and Mr. Wortley." In *Classical, Medieval and Renaissance Studies in Honor of Berthold Louis Ullman,* edited by Charles Henderson, Jr. Rome: Edigioni di Storia e Letteratura, 1964. *Tatlers* 197 and 223 are based on Wortley's notes on marriage settlements.

Brown, James. "Swift as Moralist." *Philological Quarterly* 33 (1954): 378–83. Swift as satirist and Christian.

Burt, David J. "Rakes, Rogues, and Steele's Servants." *Ball State University Forum* 11, no. 4 (1970):72–73. Suggests that the "low love" of Tom and Phillis is a satiric attack on Restoration comedy.

Carlson, C. Lennart. "Samuel Keimer." *Pennsylvania Magazine of History and Biography* 61 (1937):357–386. Keimer, Benjamin Franklin's employer, was an extravagant admirer of *The Christian Hero.*

Cohen, Michael M. "Reclamation, Revulsion, and Steele's *The Conscious Lovers*." *Restoration and Eighteenth-Century Theatre Research* 14, no. 1 (1975):23–30. Discusses flaws in *The Conscious Lovers.*

Cooke, Arthur L. "Addison vs. Steele, 1708." *PMLA* 68 (1953):313–20. Discusses the facts behind the story of Addison's loan of £1,000 to Steele.

Crane, R. S. "Suggestions Toward a Genealogy of the 'Man of Feeling.'" *English Literary History* 1 (1934):204–30. The basis of much research and publication on the latitudinarian divines and the effect of their ethical perceptions upon eighteenth-century English literature.

————. "Review Essay of William E. Alderman, 'Shaftesbury and the doctrine of moral sense in the eighteenth century,' *PMLA,* 66

(1931):1087–94." *PQ* 11 (1932):204–06. Preliminary to 1934 essay.

Dammers, Richard H. "Soldiers and Philosophers: Captain Steele and Captain Ayloffe." *Eighteenth-Century Life* 3, no. 2 (1976):52–55. On *The Christian Hero* and *The Government of the Passions*.

———. "Swift, Steele, and the Palatines: A case of Political Principle." *Ball State University Forum* 18, no. 3 (1977):17–22. Examines opposing viewpoints about the Palatines.

Dennis, John. "Remarks on a Play, Call'd, *The Conscious Lovers*, a Comedy." In *The Critical Works of John Dennis*, edited by Edward Niles Hooker. Baltimore: Johns Hopkins University Press, 1939–43. A furious attack.

Dust, Alvin I. "An Aspect of the Addison-Steele Literary Relationship." *English Language Notes* 1 (1964):196–200. Financial details.

Elliott, Robert C. "Swift's Little Harrison, Poet and Continuator of *The Tatler*." *Studies in Philology* 46 (1949):552–53. A brief summary of biographical information on Harrison.

Foxon, D. F. "A Piracy of Steele's *The Lying Lover*." *Library*, 5th ser., 10 (1955):127–29. Publication history.

Friedman, Arthur. "Goldsmith and Steele's Englishman." *Modern Language Notes* 55 (1940):294–96. Goldsmith uses *Englishman* No. 40 for 5 January 1713/14 for Letter 78 in *Citizen of the World* to describe the French.

Frye, Roland Mushat. "Swift's Yahoos and the Christian Symbols for Sin." *Journal of the History of Ideas* 15 (1954):201–217. Frye examines the traditional Christian view of human nature in the Bible and in homiletic literature.

Furlong, E. J. "How Much of Steele's *Guardian*, No. 39, Did Berkeley Write?" *Hermathena* 89 (1957):76–88. Concludes that the latter half of this paper was by Steele, not Berkeley.

Furtwangler, Albert. "The Making of Mr. Spectator." *Modern Language Quarterly* 38 (1977):21–39. Traces the refinement of the fictitious spokesmen in the *Tatler* and the *Spectator* and their development as moral authorities.

———. "Mr. Spectator, Sir Roger, and Good Humour." *University of Toronto Quarterly* 46 (1976):31–50. Discusses the origin, development, and purpose of Sir Roger de Coverly in *The Spectator*.

Green, Elvena M. "Three Aspects of Richard Steele's Theory of Comedy." *Educational Theatre Journal* 20 (1968):141–46. Excellent dramatic study.

Harkness, D. A. E. "The Opposition to the Eighth and Ninth Articles of the Commercial Treaty of Utrecht." *Scottish Historical Review* 21 (1924):219–26. Discusses opposition to the Treaty of Utrecht from commercial interests.

Hopkins, Robert H. "A Further Note on Richard Steele's Authorship of the Dedication to 'Bickerstaff's Almanack' (1709)." *Notes and Queries* 210 (1965):448–49. Steele's trouble with his creditors links him to the 1712 almanac.

———. "The Issue of Anonymity and the Beginning of the Steele-Swift Controversy of 1713–14: A New Interpretation." *English Language Notes* 2 (1964):15–21. Asserts that Steele's onslaught against Swift should be understood as motivated not by personal animosity so much as by ulterior motives of patronage.

Ito, Hiroyaki. "The Language of *The Spectator*—Chiefly Concerning the Aspect of Double-meaning." *Anglica* 5 (1962):36–62. Examines the varied connotations of selected words in *The Spectator*.

Kelsall, Malcolm. "Terence and Steele." In *The Eighteenth-Century English Stage,* edited by Richards and Thomson, pp. 11–27. London: Methuen, 1972. Both Terence and Steele explore the relationship of compassionate humane love to mere sexuality.

Kenny, Shirley Strum. "Eighteenth-Century Editions of Steele's *Conscious Lovers.*" *Studies in Bibliography* 21 (1968):253–261. Discusses three editions with the Tonson imprint dated 1723.

———. " 'Elopements, Divorce, and the Devil Knows What': Love and Marriage in English Comedy, 1690–1720." *South Atlantic Quarterly* 78 (1979):84–106.

———. "Humane Comedy." *Modern Philology* 75 (1977):29–43. Defines the shape and style of humane comedy by explaining those characteristics unique to the comedies of Steele and Farquhar, among others.

———. "Perennial Favorites: Congreve, Vanbrugh, Cibber, Farquhar, and Steele." *Modern Philology* 73, no. 4., pt. 2 (1976):54–511. Explains the considerable importance in the history of theater of drama written at the beginning of the eighteenth century.

———. "Recent Scholarship on Richard Steele." *British Studies Monitor* 10 (1973):12–24. Discusses Steele's recent emergence from the long shadow of unfriendly criticism.

———. "Steele and the 'Pattern of Genteel Comedy.' " *Modern Philology* 70 (1972):22–37. Suggests that *The Conscious Lovers* is the culmination of Steele's campaign for a new kind of drama, a "formula that was to influence generations of playwrights."

————. "Two Scenes by Addison in Steele's *Tender Husband.*" *Studies in Bibliography* 19 (1966):217–26. Argues carefully for assigning parts of Act III, scene i, and Act V, scene i, to Addison.

Kline, Richard B. "Tory Prior and Whig Steele: A Measure of Respect?" *Studies in English Literature* 9 (1969):427–37. Examines the surprising mutual respect of Steele and Prior.

Köster, Patricia. " 'Monoculus' and Party Satire." *Philological Quarterly* 49 (1970):259–62. See Henry Snyder, "The Identity of Monoculus in *The Tatler,*" *Philological Quarterly* 48 (1969):20–26, on James Ashburne.

Loftis, John. "The Blenheim Papers and Steele's Journalism, 1715–1718." *PMLA* 56 (1951):197–210. Discusses Steele manuscripts and memoranda which are preserved at Blenheim Palace and which pertain to several series of essays written between 1715 and 1718.

————. "The Genesis of Steele's *The Conscious Lovers.*" In *Essays Critical and Historical Dedicated to Lily B. Campbell,* pp. 173–82. Berkeley and Los Angeles: University of California Press, 1950. Steele began work on the plan for *The Conscious Lovers* before January, 1714, possibly as early as 1710.

————. "Richard Steele and the Drury Lane Management." *Modern Language Notes* 66 (1951):7–11. Explains the background of a letter written by the Earl of Stair from Paris in 1715 to Steele.

————. "Richard Steele, Drury Lane, and the Tories." *Modern Language Quarterly* 10 (1949):72–80. Discusses Harley's presumed attempt to woo Steele away from the Whigs.

————. "Richard Steele's Censorium." *Huntington Library Quarterly* 14 (1950):43–66. Provides a detailed account of the obscure later history of The Censorium.

————. " 'Sir John Falstaffe's' *Theatre.*" *Journal of English and Germanic Philology* 47 (1949):252–58. An account of a continuation of *The Theatre* by someone other than Steele.

————. "Steele and the Drury Lane Patent." *Modern Language Notes* 64 (1949):19–21. Argues that a memorandum of expenses preserved among the Blenheim papers refers to Steele's theatrical license, not to his patent.

Milic, Louis T. "The Reputation of Richard Steele: What Happened?" *Eighteenth-Century Life* 1, no. 4 (1975):81–87. Discusses Steele's critical reputation through the nineteenth and twentieth centuries.

————. "Tone in Steele's 'Tatler.' " *Newsletters to Newspapers: Eighteenth-Century Journalism,* edited by D. H. Bond and W. R. McLeod, pp. 33–45. Morgantown: West Virginia University, 1977. Discusses the relationship of the writer to the reader in the *Tatler*.

Moore, C. A. "Shaftesbury and the Ethical Poets in England, 1700–1760." *PMLA* 31 (1916):264–325. Discusses the literary influence of Shaftesbury's *Characteristics*.

Moore, John Robert. "Defoe, Steele, and the Demolition of Dunkirk." *Huntington Library Quarterly* 13 (1950):279–302. Provides an illuminating review of the importance of the demolition of Dunkirk as an issue in English journalism.

————. "Gildon's Attack on Steele and Defoe in *The Battle of the Authors*." *PMLA* 66 (1951):534–38. Argues for Gildon's authorship of this anonymous tract of 1720.

————. "Steele's Unassigned Tract against the Earl of Oxford." *Philological Quarterly* 28 (1949):413–18. Appears in appendix to *Tracts and Pamphlets*.

Needham, Gwendolyn B. "Mrs. Manley: An Eighteenth-Century Wife of Bath." *Huntington Library Quarterly* 14 (1950):259–84. Manley may have been Steele's mistress and certainly became his enemy.

Novak, Maximillian E. "The Sentimentality of *The Conscious Lovers* Revisited and Reasserted." *Modern Language Studies* 9, no. 3 (Fall, 1979):48–59. Asserts that sentimental rather than exemplary is the correct description of Steele's plays.

Parnell, Paul E. "The Etiquette of the Sentimental Repentance Scene, 1688–96." *Papers in Language and Literature* 14 (1978):205–17. Examines the repentance scene in comedy after 1688 and suggests that there is greater psychological complexity than previous criticism has indicated.

————. "A New Molière Scene for Steele's *The Tender Husband*." *Notes and Queries* 204 (1959):218. The inventory of goods left to Biddy Tipkin (V, ii) and Harpagon's inventory in *L'Avare* (II, i).

————. "A Source for the Duel Scene in *The Conscious Lovers*." *Notes and Queries* 207 (1962):13–15. Suggests Cibber's *Woman's Wit*.

Paulissen, Mary Nelson. "Richard Steele's *The Conscious Lovers*: The Use of the Doppelgänger." *American Imago: A Psychoanalytic Journal for Culture, Science, and the Arts* 35 (1978):419–30. *The Conscious Lovers* shows evidence of having been written from Steele's unconscious desire to create a *Shutzgeist,* a good double, which would represent the virtuous qualities that the *Doppelgänger,* or dark side of Steele's nature, did not possess.

Potter, George R. "Swift and Natural Science." *Philological Quarterly* 20 (1941):97–118. Discusses the extent and the sources of Swift's knowledge of science. Cf. review by Louis A. Landa, *PQ* 21 (1942):219–21.

Rau, Fritz. "Zum Gehalt des *Tatler* und *Spectator.*" *Anglia* 88 (1970):42–93. A very full survey and appraisal of research on the content of the essays. The principal categories considered are literary criticism, aesthetics, morals, social reform, and history of ideas.

Reynolds, Richard R. "The Fall and Rise of Richard Steele: A Crossroads of Law and Politics." *Enlightenment Essays* 4, nos. 3–4 (1973):36–41. Discusses the question of a citizen's freedom to comment adversely on the government and Steele's place in that controversy in 1714.

Rogers, Pat. "A New Letter by Steele: The Earl of Nottingham and *The Conscious Lovers.*" *English Language Notes* 7 (1969):105–07. Letter from Steele to Nottingham, 16 Jan. 1722, enlisting his support for the play and suggesting that Nottingham had aided Steele in his efforts to obtain the Drury Lane patent in 1714/15.

Smith, John Harrington. "Tony Lumpkin and the Country Booby Type in Antecedent English Comedy." *PMLA* 58 (1943):1038–49. Suggests connections among Humphry Gubbin, Tony Lumpkin, and earlier country booby types.

Snyder, Henry L. "Arthur Maynwaring, Richard Steele, and *The Lives of Two Illustrious Generals.*" *Studies in Bibliography* 24 (1971):152–62. Detailed and useful research.

————. "The Circulation of Newspapers in the Reign of Queen Anne." *Library,* 5th ser., 23 (1968):217. Provides considerable data on the newspaper circulation, "derived from the tax records of stamped paper bought by the newspaper printers for the last two years of Anne's reign."

————. "The Identity of Monoculus in *The Tatler.*" *Philological Quarterly* 48 (1969):20–26. James Ashburne, a gambler, was also known as Sir James of the Peak.

Staves, Susan. "Liars and Lying in Alarcón, Corneille, and Steele." *Revue de littérature comparée* 46 (1972):514–27. Examines the difference between Steele's *The Lying Lover* and its sources, namely in treatment of lying and in sentimentality.

Stephens, John C., Jr. "Mr. Crab, the Librarian." *Notes and Queries* 201 (1956):105–06. Identifies a character in the *Guardian* No. 60 as Under-keeper of the Bodleian Library.

———. "Steele and the Bishop of St. Asaph's Preface." *PMLA* 67 (1952):1011–23. Discusses *Spectator* No. 384, which threw political neutrality to the winds.

———. "Steele Quotes Two Great Divines." *Notes and Queries* 201 (1956):252–53. Refers to quotations in the *Guardian* from Tillotson and William Beveridge.

Thomas, Joseph M. "Swift and the Stamp Act of 1712." *PMLA* 31 (1916):247–63. Discusses Swift's responsibility regarding the Stamp Act.

Todd, William B. "Early Editions of *The Tatler.*" *Studies in Bibliography* 15 (1962):121–33. Examines textual variants.

Winton, Calhoun. "Addison and Steele in the English Enlightenment." *Studies on Voltaire and the Eighteenth Century,* vol. 27, edited by T. Besterman (Geneva: Institute et Museé Voltaire, 1963), 1901–1918. Steele's optimism about improving the state of human existence.

———. "New Documents concerning Richard Steele's Father." *Journal of English and Germanic Philology* 58 (1959):264–69. Steele's father was a lawyer in Dublin.

———. "Richard Steele, Journalist—and Journalism." *Newsletters to Newspapers: Eighteenth-Century Journalism,* edited by D. H. Bond and W. R. McLeod, pp. 21–31. Morgantown: West Virginia University, 1977. Discusses the relationship between journalism and literature.

———. "Steele and the Fall of Harley in 1714." *Philological Quarterly* 37 (1958):440–47. Discusses Steele's Whig ideals and their effect on his journalism.

———. "Steele, Mrs. Manley, and John Lacey." *Philological Quarterly* 42 (1963):272–75. Argues that Lacey is indeed not the author of *The Ecclesiastical History of Whig-Land.*

———. "Steele, Swift, and the Queen's Physician." In *The Augustan Milieu: Essays Presented to Louis A. Landa,* edited by Miller, Rothstein, Rousseau, pp. 138–54. Oxford: Clarendon Press, 1970. An illuminating account of Sir David Hamilton's journal.

———. "Steele, the Junto and *The Tatler* No. 4." *Modern Language Notes* 72 (1957):178–82. Explains the political significance of the allegorical propaganda for the Whig Junto in *Tatler* 4, 19 April 1709.

3. Dissertations

Blanchard, Rae. "Richard Steele as a Moralist and Social Reformer." Diss. University of Chicago, 1927. An outstanding and pioneering study of Steele's moral position.

Cameron, Ruth A. "The Prose Style of Addison and Steele in the Periodical Essay." Diss. Boston University, 1972. This dissertation analyzes the periodical essays in order to isolate any observable differences in their styles.

Carter, Charlotte A. "Personae and Characters in the Essays of Addison, Steele, Fielding, Johnson, and Goldsmith." Diss. University of Denver, 1969. This dissertation examines the persona and the character sketch in various essays.

Hall, Elmo Murray. "Richard Steele: A Conscious Rationalist." Diss. Oklahoma State University, 1974. Argues against Rae Blanchard's perception of Steele's fundamentally irrational concept of human nature.

Kenny, Shirley Strum. "An Edition of Richard Steele's *The Funeral* and *The Tender Husband*." Diss. University of Chicago, 1964. The basis for Professor Kenny's edition of all of the plays.

McCleary, Willard Clark. "An Analysis of Swift's Quarrel with Steele, 1710–14." Diss. University of Denver, 1975. "Throughout the whole of this study an effort has been made to sympathetically view Swift on a personal level as the aggrieved rather than an instigator of that impasse which brought about the severance of friendly relations between himself and Steele" (Preface).

Marshall, Madeleine. "Sentimental Drama in England, France, and Germany: a fresh view of the 'rational choice and moral conduct' components, as reinforced by the theory and practice of natural acting in the eighteenth century." Diss. New York University, 1973. Discusses *The Conscious Lovers* as exemplary drama in section on Steele.

Tatton, John Francis. "Richard Steele and Terence." Diss. University of Texas, 1970. Discusses Terence's influence upon Steele.

Webster, Ernest Rogers. "The Evolving Critical Reputation of Richard Steele's Role in the *Tatler*." Diss. Ball State University, 1970. This study describes the critical reputation of Richard Steele's role in the *Tatler* as it has evolved through three centuries, from Steele's own time to 1965.

Index

DATE DUE

GAYLORD			PRINTED IN U.S.A.